DEMONS ARE

REAL!

Journey with me as I expose Hell

Equipping you for Battle

By

Mark A. Couch

Demons Are Real, by Mark A. Couch

ISBN # 978-1-936937-96-7

For More Information:

Markcouchministries.com

info@couchmediagroup.com

Demonsarereal.org

Po box 830

Fairburn, GA 30213

Dedication

Sometimes success is predicated upon the village and support system that surrounds you. There are several key people that God put in place to under gird and support my family and me during this most difficult season. My mother, Mariann Couch, in-laws, Dr. Shirley Redd and Judge Edward Redd, sister-in-laws, Sara and Rachel Redd.

As a village, they were always there to assist with the children and pray even when they were not sure exactly what we were dealing with. I would also like to thank the Lifeline Church family that remained steadfast amidst my inconsistency. Thank you for your prayers and being in place at all times.

Lastly, but most importantly, I want to thank God for the beautiful wife he gave me to travel this road with. Every test we have had to endure only caused us to fall deeper in love. I thank you Ivy for your love, strength, faith and willingness to share your story with the world.

Table of Contents

Introduction:

My Story 11

Demons in the Darkness 15

Can Christians be Possessed? 20

14 Months of Hell 26

Deliverance and Healing 36

Satan's Plan and Operation 41

The Danger of Psychics 49

Your Religious Prayer Won't Work 55

Ready For War 62

Fighting With the Devil 73

Demons in My House 81

Queen of Hell 90

Take Authority.................................105

Conclusion: 111

Introduction

Writing this book was a true challenge due to the fact that we now live in a time where Christianity has become increasingly unpopular. Traditional Christians are deemed to be narrow-minded, too deep, or unwilling to embrace the world and other religions that conflict with our faith. I never thought I would live in a day, as a pastor, where I must be cognizant of all public statements; having to censor what I say in efforts of not offending.

Statistics say the majority of Christians, more-less non-Christians, don't believe in Satan and demons. For years I kept my knowledge and experiences with demons suppressed for fear of being marginalized and placed in a box. My challenge extended beyond the pulpit into the secular arena. The question and concern became, 'what will colleagues and associates think?' Will they be spooked, or simply consider me weird and out of touch?

When I entered into ministry, I experienced firsthand the feeling of isolation. I was not ready to relive that experience again knowing this time it would be on a much greater scale and platform. In other words, demons are very smart. When they know you have the power to cast them out, they will do all they can to sever that relationship. Demons work hard to remove people from around you that put them in danger of eviction.

(Ephesians 6:12) "For we do not wrestle against flesh and blood, but against principalities, against powers, against the rulers of the darkness of this age, against spiritual hosts of wickedness in the heavenly places."

(Luke 10:19) "Behold, I give you the authority to trample on serpents and scorpions, and over all the power of the enemy, and nothing shall by any means hurt you."

There are portions of this book where I discuss my experiences and disclose what I vowed to keep a secret. Some will read and say to themselves, "No way." Others who are more knowledgeable about demons and deliverance will believe and understand. Either way, I am excited now and the fear is gone! Through God's grace I am equipped and ready to push back the gates of Hell and pull down every stronghold. Journey with me as I expose Hell and equip you for a battle!

Chapter I

My Story

Anybody who knew me growing up, whether it was a family member, teammate, band member, someone from the club or someone from the streets, would have never predicted I would become a pastor; more less one versed in deliverance. I will never forget in 1995, when a lady came in my record store and prophesied I would become a pastor. I thought it was hilarious. I laughed in her face. Assuming she was mentally off, I said to her, "With divine intervention, I might be in a choir, but never a pastor." A few weeks later her husband, a childhood friend of mine, gave me a book to read entitled, "Divine Revelation of Hell." It left a lasting impact on my perception of hell. I heard pastors talk about going to heaven and hell but not about demons. Outside of what my mother, a Sunday school teacher, shared with me about hell and demons, I knew nothing. Therefore, the vivid depiction of hell and demons portrayed in the book stuck with me, and for a while scared the hell out of me. I had no idea the demons that scared me then would fear me now.

People often ask what led me into deliverance. All I can say is, it was not calculated. When I was 19, three years before the pastoring prophecy, I worked in an adult entertainment club. Since I spent a lot of time clubbing in my teenage years, I deemed this to be the job of a lifetime. I was under age, getting paid, and surrounded by exposed women. However, being spiritually blind and dead, I had no idea that for eight hours a day, five days a week I was literally in the Devil's playhouse. Today, I look back and praise God He kept me and what I was blind to then I can see now. Even though I've had many other instances of sin and depravity, I'll put them all together now realizing sometimes God will allow us to be exposed and privy to certain diabolical environments and situations so that in the future our light will shine in the midst of the very darkness that should have killed us.

(Luke 22:31-32) "And the Lord said, "Simon, Simon! Indeed, Satan has asked for you, that he may sift you as wheat. But I have prayed for you; that your faith should not fail; and

when you have returned to me, strengthen your brethren."

In this passage of scripture, Jesus allowed Satan to attack Peter, but he informed Peter that he prayed his faith would not fail. This meant he would survive the attack but only by God's grace so he could walk in his purpose. Then he stated 'when you make it through, go back and strengthen your brother'; speaking of those who would suffer the same tribulation, attack and treatment. I'm telling you child of God, the storm is not there to tear you down. Rather, it is there to build you and your witnessing.

In 1996, I started back attending church and in 1998 in the midst of sin, God continuously gave me visions and dreams about pastoring and preaching. During this season, I developed this unusual thirst for God. Three to five days a week I was in church; Methodist churches, Deliverance churches, Baptist churches, and non-denominational churches. Being young with no biases, I was able to pull something from all of the churches I frequented. I was most intrigued by pastors who believed and operated in healing and deliverance. Eventually, I became an associate minister under the leadership of one of Atlanta's prominent ministers. He afforded me the freedom of finding my way. In other words, I was all over the place. Anointed with no theological training or direction made me a loose cannon. Whatever preacher I was listening to that week, that's who I became. One month I was prophesying, the next month deliverance, and the next month healing. But, even amidst my spiritual schizophrenia, God had his hand on me and it was simply beginners' training for a rookie in the kingdom.

In 2002, I launched my own church while finishing bible college. By this time I had read many books on deliverance and experienced several deliverance services. Even though I launched a traditional Baptist Church, deliverance played a major role. All of a sudden the training was a little more intense and the unseen realm more visible.

Notes

Chapter II

Demons in the Darkness

Anything that is in darkness is hidden until it is exposed by the light. Scripture teaches us that Satan is pompous and prideful but he hides in darkness to veil his mission.

(Isaiah 14:12) "How you are fallen from heaven, O Lucifer, son of the morning! How you are cut down to the ground, you who weakened the nations! 13 for you have said in your heart; 'I will ascend into heaven, I will exalt my throne above the stars of God; I will also sit on the mount of the congregation on the farthest sides of the north; 14 I will ascend above the heights of the clouds, I will be like the Most High."

Again, pride is the main reason behind Satan's fall from heaven but oxymoronically he seeks to remain hidden and covert. The last thing the enemy wants is for you to believe he exists. When doing a study, I was shocked at the number of Christians who don't believe in hell or the devil. The latest polling done within the last 10 years disclosed that 60% of Christians don't believe in the devil and 30% don't believe in hell. This explains why so many churches lack power. You just can't fight what you don't believe exists.

In 2015, during an off the record interview with a prominent pastor that turned into a theological debate, I was dumbfounded to hear this man who presently pastors a thriving Baptist Church in Atlanta state he didn't believe in heaven, hell, demons or the divinity of Christ. In this church they shout and dance every week. No one knows their pastor is, for the most part, an atheist, preaching from a Bible he doesn't believe to be the inerrant, irrefutable Word of God. Churches with this type of leadership manufacture weekly services that are religious and emotional but lack the power to cause transformation and freedom from bondage. In essence, I am telling you, you can be saved and shout and still be bound by the enemy. I will speak more on this in the chapter, "Can a Christian be Possessed?"

Contrary to popular belief, you can not shout demons out.

In my experience many of the ones that danced and shouted the most needed the most deliverance. Even I went through periods and seasons when I would shout, dance and remain bound. For example, have you ever been to an amusement park with your children, got on a roller coaster and hated the entire experience? The up and down, side to side, jerking and pulling but knew the ride wouldn't last long so you endured till the end? Well that's how the demonic spirits feel when they are abiding in someone saved and sanctified but not delivered. They hate your hands going up, the falling to your knees, running, dancing, screaming and shouting. They will endure a good shout, a good dance, a good praise break knowing that it will soon come to an end. In most cases the demons know they will get a full six day reprieve before you come back to church and shout again. Spirits don't mind you feeling free two or three hours a week in exchange for a place to call home. The truth is, they would rather be uncomfortable for a few hours than homeless! They keep hiding out, wanting you to believe you are just a regular person with issues that you must simply live with and temper. Please don't get me wrong. I believe in praising God in the midst of affliction. But it makes a difference when you shout, praise and dance knowing Christ died for you to be free.

(Psalm 34:19) "Many are the afflictions of the righteous, but the LORD delivers him out of them all." (John 10:10) "The thief does not come except to steal, and to kill, and to destroy. I have come that they may have life, and that they may have it more abundantly."

If this Word is currently ministering to your spirit, do not let another minute pass without making a faith declaration! With the fruit of your lips decree breakthrough and deliverance in the name of Jesus! It is not the Will of God for you to pretend to be free outwardly and bound inwardly. If life and death is in the power of the tongue, use your mouth to speak life! For whom the Son has set free is free indeed!

Let's pray. "Jesus I accept you into my heart and I believe in your life, death and resurrection. I ask that you fill me with your Holy Spirit. Anything in me that's not like you uncover it, unveil it, open my eyes, help me to see in the spirit. Open my ears so I can hear your voice. Guide my steps so I can go where you've called me to go. Expose every enemy and demonic spirit that dwells in darkness that hides in wait. Anoint me fresh with the wisdom and discernment needed to prevail and overcome the enemy of my soul. Help me to walk in the victory you won for me on the cross." Amen!

Notes

Chapter III

Can Christians be Possessed?

In church, Bible College and seminary, I was taught the same theology in regards to salvation. (Romans 10:9) *"If you confess with your mouth the Lord Jesus and believe in your heart that God has raised Him from the dead, you will be saved."* This scripture tells us that once you confess and believe you are saved! Salvation literally means to be delivered from the power and penalty of sin. Now when you are saved, it is then the Holy Spirit comes on the inside of you.

(II Corinthians 1:21-22) "Now He who establishes us with you in Christ and has anointed us is God, who also has sealed us and given us the Spirit in our hearts as a guarantee."

(Ephesians 1:13-14) "In Him you also trusted, after you heard the word of truth, the gospel of your salvation; in whom also, having believed, you were sealed with the Holy Spirit of promise, who is the guarantee of our inheritance until the redemption of the purchased possession, to the praise of His glory."

Considering these scriptures, many theologians and denominational leaders have concluded that the Holy Spirit indwells believers at the point of salvation. In turn, demonic spirits cannot inhabit the same temple. This means you cannot be saved and be under the control of a demonic spirit. This is what I dogmatically believed and Jesus knows I defended this Baptist leaning position from the pulpit and beyond. I dared someone to challenge me believing whole-heartedly that any other doctrine was not sound and misleading. The more robust version of this theological position has a Pentecostal lean. This belief system suggests that not only must you believe with your heart and confess with your mouth that God raised Christ from the grave and that Jesus is Lord to be saved, but you must also be filled with the Holy Ghost with evidence of speaking in tongues to prove it.

Let me share with you my current position and what changed my prior theological position that I so passionately defended. I found my current position by merging both positions mentioned. I ended up with a sound Bible based conclusion that closely parallels the Full Gospel Theological Doctrine. My current position is, I don't believe you need to be filled with the spirit to be saved. I do believe you need to be filled with the spirit in order to be free from demonic infiltration. Before you close the book, let me explain from my experience validated by the Word.

At the church I started and pastored, at the conclusion of most sermons I would often do altar calls. Even though I was not completely versed in deliverance, I could discern when someone was under demonic attack. As I collectively prayed for people who were suicidal, suffering with addictions and other forms of affliction, some would pass out or start to convulse violently. I then started to pray for those people individually. This led to full-fledged deliverance and needless to say, some extended church services. My concern and befuddlement was that the people I was delivering were in leadership! Praise dancers, choir members, people I knew had accepted Christ into their heart and were saved!

I started asking God and myself the question, 'How can these people be saved, on fire, dancing, praising, singing and have a demonic spirit in them?' This baffled me for months. I didn't get it! After seeing this in deliverance time and time again, it was clear to me that saved people can be infiltrated by demons. What finalized this position was a direct conversation with a demon while doing deliverance. You may be wondering how this is possible. Let me explain. Before you can truly cast out ruling spirits, strongholds or generational demons, you must get the spirit to identify him or herself. Demons fight to the end to keep from being identified. Once they respond to the command, "Say your name," the door is also open for conversation proposing questions such as: "How did you enter? When did you enter? What gave you access? How long have you been here and who else is with you?"

When I started doing deliverance, I didn't know we had authority to go this far. Once the demon reluctantly identified him or herself, I would immediately command the spirit to come out by name. (You will learn more about this in the chapter, "Take Authority." The conclusion is, you can be saved and still be infiltrated by evil spirits. My theological position is, once you have accepted Christ into your heart and receive salvation, you must then ask God to fill you with His power and spirit. Faith and power from the Holy Ghost must take over so there will be no room for the enemy to dwell in you. We are all tempted by the devil. We all experience warfare in the mind, but it is one thing to be oppressed by the devil and another to be possessed by the devil. Over time I learned to discern the difference between the two. I found that some people are suppressed by the enemy, meaning they have succumbed to doubt and fear. They believe the diabolical thoughts of failure and defeat implanted in their minds by the enemy. Then there are others who are completely depressed and overcome by the enemy. At times they take on the personality of the very demon they are being infiltrated by. As a result, they become suicidal and in some cases self-mutilate. The latter are those who have been possessed by the demonic spirits, and thus, unable to control their behavior and actions.

Let me give you a few examples. In 2004, my grandfather, who was a long time active member of his church, committed suicide by shooting himself in the head. The week prior, the state confiscated his driver's license. He was so depressed. I can hear the enemy whispering to him, "You're not a man anymore; your life is ruined. Now you must depend on others for the rest of your life." My grandfather was very prideful, stubborn, and independent. The enemy used the character flaw of pride as an avenue to take over his mind.

Around 2008, there was a woman who attended my church that was young, beautiful, and vibrant. She had two children. She seemed to be happy with life. But, one Sunday I asked those who were depressed and considering suicide to raise their hands. I noticed from the pulpit that her hand slightly went up. I then asked all who raised their hands to come down to the altar. While others came down and were set free, she stayed in her seat. I assumed she was touched by the corporate prayer and perhaps felt better. The following week she committed suicide in the same manner as my grandfather. This hurt me to the core; but again, both situations taught me how demons can quickly work through depression, take over the mind and cause a believer to become suicidal. There are other examples of possession of which I will discuss in the next chapter, "14 Months of Hell."

Let's pray. God in the name of Jesus, I pray that you will remove all fear from my life. I thank you for the power that you have given me to take authority over hell and the powers therein. I will not succumb to fear and depression! The devil will not win my mind! God I asked now that you will fill me with your power, with your anointing, with your Holy Spirit. Fortify my faith; help my non-belief so that through faith and power I will keep the devil under my feet! Amen

Notes

Chapter IV

"14 Months of Hell"

I had no idea that my time at my church was preparing me to perform exorcisms. This consisted of intense direct contact with demons, which at times can become physically and mentally exhausting. Over the years, I learned a lot through study and various experiences. Nothing could totally prepare me for what was to come. The most traumatic experience of my life was having to deliver my best friend and lover; that being my wife. (My eyes are welling with tears as I write.)

I met Ivy in 2009. After our first outing together in November 2009, we were engaged Christmas Day and married on May 22, 2010. She was pregnant three months later. My wife had a condition whereby she lived in pain close to three weeks out of every month. She was only completely pain-free ten or so days after her menstrual cycle. During the pregnancy, the pain subsided but afterwards it started again. She was constantly taking pain pills for relief and I was getting concerned. We prayed for healing and believed but the pain never left. We just accepted the situation and dealt with it the best we could.

In 2012, we were cast to be on a national reality show called, "The Sisterhood" Aka "The Preachers Wives of Atlanta." With Ivy experiencing constant pain, the filming, at times, was overly taxing to say the least. Over time it got to the point where we could no longer hide her situation. During the course of the show, we went to the emergency room several times and ended up talking to a specialist that believed she suffered with endometriosis. Surgery was recommended, not ruling out the possible need for a hysterectomy.

(Endometriosis (en-doe-me-tree-o-sis) is an often painful disorder in which tissue that normally lines the inside of your uterus; the endometrial grows outside your uterus. Endometriosis most commonly involves the ovaries, fallopian tubes and the tissue lining the pelvis. Hysterectomy is the surgical removal of the uterus. In a total hysterectomy, the uterus, ovaries and cervix are removed. In some cases, the fallopian tubes. Needless to say, the network and producers desperately wanted to capture everything on camera and make the surgery a part of our story line. Being that reality TV is supposed to be reality, we agreed to allow the cameras to capture our experience. With the approval of the hospital and the surgical doctor in charge, it became our storyline on national TV.

On the week of surgery, Ivy's mother, a retired anesthesiologist, flew in town. On the day of surgery we were concerned but optimistic. We hoped the surgery would reveal the source of Ivy's horrific pain. We were also prayerful that if they found something it would not mean what the doctors warned us about; that being Ivy would be unable to have any more children. The goal of the doctor was to go in and remove any tissue or abnormalities that could be causing pain. After the surgery was over, surrounded by cameras, the doctor comes to me saying he saw no abnormalities and everything looked great. We all gave praise to God believing prayers were answered and she was healed of her affliction.

For three to four months everything was wonderful, no pain just a normal life. Late 2012, the pain came back and worse. We did not want to tell anyone because we had proclaimed healing. We felt it would look bad if people knew we were right back in the same situation. We suffered silently trying to hide the affliction from friends and family. August 2013, Ivy was pregnant with our second child and like before during the pregnancy the pain subsided. A few months after giving birth, we were right back in the same situation. I felt helpless watching as she curled up in pain day after day. Some thought she was exaggerating. I knew she wasn't faking (Lord Help me my eyes are filling with tears as I relive the agony). This pain was real! When the pain would come, she would cry and scream in agony often times saying, "Mark, I just want to die! Please help!" It made no sense to me. At church I was praying for people, doing deliverance and many were being healed and set free. Then I would come home to a wife suffering and no matter how much I prayed nothing changed. In secret I cried out to God saying, "How could you allow this beautiful loving woman, who is known for her love and compassion to suffer so violently? How can you use me to deliver and heal others but not the one I love?" You will hear more about ineffective prayer in the chapter, "Your Religious Prayers Won't Work." It was horrible! Day after day, week after week, the pain would come and go. Just about every Sunday we were late for church because many of the pain attacks consistently showed up on Sunday morning. Many times, Ivy had to leave during service and vomit just to calm her stomach. We were both tired and frustrated sexually, emotionally, spiritually, mentally and physically. The problem was that neither of us knew things would get unbelievably worse before they got better.

One night Ivy and I were watching television. I can't remember what we were watching but after the program went off something prompted her to share with me a deep secret from her past. I'll never forget the moment, it was tense. I assumed I knew everything about her. I could not imagine what she was about to say. She began to confide in me and express that at a very young age, being in the wrong environment with trusted people, she was repeatedly exposed to pornography. I knew she had not lived a promiscuous life. In fact, she remained a virgin until 29 years of age and was raised well by her parents. However, at a young age she was subjected to hours upon hours of filth that over the years resulted in emotional bondade destroying the innocence of her young mind. This diabolical exposure created a lustful desire to watch pornography. With images and scenes etched in her mind, it took away major parts of her childhood innocence. This caught me off guard being that we never watched or entertained pornography. She explained how the experience made her more prudent as an adult causing her to work hard at making sure what she felt inwardly was not displayed outwardly. It hurt me to my core when she expressed that she was fearful and ashamed to share her pain with me believing I would leave her. Again, a

29

prime example of how demonic strongholds will work through shame and fear to keep someone from opening up about their dark places. Something that night initiated the conversation and she began to empty her heart passionately with tears. I could tell that simultaneously, weight was being lifted off her. Not only was she cleansing, she was also uncovering and exposing demons that sought to remain hidden.

As she spoke, my spiritual antennas went up. Through experience and study, I knew pornography was a portal through which demons could gain access to one's life. The eyes and ears are gateways to the heart and the heart is easily polluted. Once the heart is polluted, it affects our mind and thought process. Once our thought process is polluted we say and act on what we think.

(Proverbs 4:23) "Keep your heart with all diligence, for out of it spring the issues of life".

(Jeremiah 17:9) "The heart is deceitful above all things, and desperately wicked."

As she cried, she asked me to pray. I held her and commenced with a general prayer. As I prayed, she cried more profusely. I started to pray more specifically, asking God to deliver her from demonic oppression and hurt. The prayer went something like this: "I come against every demonic force that has sought to attack her mind and body. I plead the blood of Jesus over her and asked God to set her free by His power." After about twenty minutes of praying in the spirit and in the natural what happened next caught me off guard and for a moment pumped fear into my veins. Ivy's eyes began to roll in her head, her face became pale, her voice changed and she pushed me away. Let me be honest. Even though I conducted many deliverance services and casted out many demons, it was always with two or more people involved or in the midst of a church service. I never encountered a demon face-to-face in close quarters, let alone, at my house in my bedroom. Initially, I wanted to leave the room but love made me stay and the Holy Spirit spoke to my heart with this scripture:

(Luke 10:19) "Behold, I give you the authority to trample on serpents and scorpions, and over all the power of the enemy, and nothing shall by any means hurt you."

Immediately I felt power and fear was replaced with boldness and tenacity. I began to pray more in the spirit and spoke directly to the demonic spirit. I commanded the demon saying, "Look me in the eyes and speak your name." The more I demanded, the more violent the situation became. At one point I found myself holding Ivy down on the bed and it literally took all my strength. I am 6'3, 235lb and I bench press 350lb. At times, it took all I had to keep her 5'2, 132lb body down. Eventually the spirit named itself as, "Kill Her." I said, "In the name of Jesus who died for our sins, I command you to come out!" I did this over and over. Then the spirit let out a loud long scream! Ivy started coughing and I knew she was delivered. After a few minutes, Ivy returned to normal with energy knowing a weight was lifted. Neither of us could believe what had just happened. She was not aware of all of her actions. She just knew something was wrong. Typically, when someone is being delivered they literally lose control. Their body is overtaken by the Spirit, an internal fight ensues, and the enemy suppresses the personality and will power of their victim, completely taking over their body, mind and emotions. Some people call this blacking out. It's not a black out, rather, it's a takeover by evil spirits.

After this experience was over, we began to give God praise thinking that was it. It wasn't. The very next day Ivy had a severe pain attack. Lying on her back, she started violently tossing from side to side clinging to her stomach. From the last experience, I knew Ivy was under attack and this pain was not being caused by natural problems or identifiable elements. This was a spirit! I got down on my knees, laid one hand on her

31

stomach, the other on her head and I started praying in the spirit. From the last experience, I remembered this really irritated the evil spirit. As before, all of a sudden it was not her anymore. I went through the same process commanding the spirit saying, "What is your name?" In a low groan the spirit said, "Vashti." Vashti is a female demonic spirit that attacks only women. It takes up residence in the womb causing dull and sharp pains throughout the day. This time instead of immediately casting the spirit out in a stern commanding tone I said, "How did you gain access to her body?" The spirit responded saying "Television." The conversation ensued and I was able to find out when the spirit entered, how it entered, and the person Ivy was with that exposed her to pornography. I then commanded the spirit to come out and immediately her pain went away. Instantly Ivy felt miraculous relief. I started to tell her about the conversation and what I learned through it. In disbelief, she confirmed everything I shared with her was true. At this moment, I knew why the doctors were not able to find anything. Even though they gave her condition several names of what they thought it could have been, nothing was resolved. Through experience, I have come to learn when doctors cannot figure out what exactly is going on with a patient, the incurable condition that can only be controlled or managed is given a name.

Ivy felt great for a few weeks. Then one night around 2AM, I was awakened by her tossing back and forth in her sleep while simultaneously moaning in fear. She was having a nightmare that caused physical reaction and manifestation. Many people at some point in their life experience have nightmares where they are being attacked in their sleep. Perhaps you know what I am referring to. Have you ever had a nightmare in which you were being choked, chased, smothered or held down and after the nightmare was over, or in the midst of it you woke up in a cold sweat, gasping for air, heart pumping, trying to catch your breath? Even though you were sleep in an unconscious state, what you experienced was real. Let me say it another way. You were being attacked spiritually but it manifested physically, or, everything you felt physically even though you were unconscious was happening spiritually. Meaning you were attacked by evil spirits that operate in the unseen spiritual realm possessing the power to inflict physical damage. Remember, "We wrestle not against flesh and blood." Consider this story found in Acts 19:13-16.

"*13 Then some of the itinerant Jewish exorcists took it upon themselves to call the name of the Lord Jesus over those who had evil spirits, saying, "We exorcise you by the Jesus whom Paul preaches." 14 Also there were seven sons of Sceva, a Jewish chief priest, who did so. 15 And the evil spirit answered and said, "Jesus I know, and Paul I know; but who are you?" 16 Then the man in whom the evil spirit was leaped on them, overpowered them, and prevailed against them, so that they fled out of that house naked and wounded."*

This story discloses evil spirits that could not be seen attacked these men causing physical damage that was visible. In like manner, Ivy experienced an attack in the unseen realm that caused physical pain and discomfort. The difference was when she woke up the attack continued. Again, she started tossing and turning violently in pain. I went through the exact same process as before and after a full two hours the spirit identified itself as "Torture." This spirit was causing the violent pain in her stomach. It was not endometriosis, severe cramps, gas or anything else she was diagnosed with. Rather, it was demonic spirits attacking her organs. Sometimes when doctors can't detect and see the cause of pain, but know something is wrong, it's simply because evil spirits do not show up on X-rays and MRI's. In like manner, not all mental disorders can be cured with medicine. Rather, there are many people with personality and mental disorders that need deliverance. Throughout the gospels, Jesus delivered people that lost control of their mind and emotions due to demonic attack.

(Matthew 4:24) "Then His fame went throughout all

Syria; and they brought to Him all sick people who were afflicted with various diseases and torments, and those who were demon-possessed, epileptics, and paralytics; and He healed them."

We endured this situation for 14 months. Every week there was a series of attacks and deliverance. All of this with two babies, a growing church, yet Ivy still loved on others and wore a smile. Even though we both can attest it was the worst time of our lives, we recognize the pain and trials brought us even closer together, trained us and gave us insight into the spiritual realm no person or book could have ever taught us. Little did we know that God was only preparing us for what was to come.

Let's Pray. God I thank you that there is purpose attached to my pain and that what didn't kill me will only make me stronger. So God be glorified, be glorified! In my heart! In my mind! Through these trials and tribulation have your way! I bless you in advance knowing that all things are working for my good. Amen!

Notes

Chapter V

Deliverance and Healing

After the 14 months of what I deemed intense warfare training, I entered into a season of deliverance and healing at my church. I was empowered by the experience but also disgusted by demons. I hated the fact that I now knew without reservation many people were suffering due to demonic oppression. For example, I knew people who felt worthless or insecure wasn't just having emotional swings. From sicknesses to generational curses I could discern demonic affliction and I was determined to set as many people free as possible. I spent weeks discussing angelology, demonology, pneumatology and theology all in an effort to help Christian's understand Satan's kingdom and how we have been given authority by way of the cross to defeat hell.

(Luke 10:19) "Behold, I give unto you power to tread on serpents and scorpions, and over all the power of the enemy: and nothing shall by any means hurt you."

After the 14 month ordeal, I learned something very valuable. There is a difference between being taught and experience. In seminary and Bible College, I studied and learned about all of the theologies, dispensation, history, the life and ministry of Christ, you name it. I thank God for Christian education. I believe every pastor and teacher of God's word should pursue it. If ever given the ultimatum of choosing between the two, I would have to go with experience. Albeit school taught me about God, my experiences showed me God. It's one thing to be taught about angels and demons, light and darkness, good and evil. It's another thing to see it, experience it and live through it. Living in this day and time when the majority of Christians don't believe the Bible is literal and that Satan and hell is real, my experience undergirds and tells me no matter what the world says or what people think I know without doubt and trepidation that heaven is real, hell is real, Satan is real, God is real and "Demons are real."

Even though I veered away, I started back doing altar calls at church that led to healing and deliverance. Out of the many miracles I will never forget the case of a young man in my church, a 14 year old born with sickle cell. This child stayed in pain and his single mother was constantly taking him back and forth to the hospital. His situation was so grave he was contacted by the "Make a Wish Foundation" who allows children to make a dying request that they grant. One weekend I was informed by the mother that he needed an immediate blood transfusion set to take place on a Monday or Tuesday. I encouraged her to please get him to church on Sunday before the transfusion. That Sunday, we did an altar call and his mother brought him down for prayer. When I got to him I could sense and feel the presence of God. I gently laid my hands on his head and began to plead the blood of Jesus commanding the spirit of death to leave his life. He fell straight back lying on the floor motionless (kids don't fake this).

While he was on the floor I stated that God was giving him a blood transfusion; replacing his tainted blood with the blood of the Lamb. The next day she took him to the hospital to receive the transfusion. Following protocol, before they could start the process they had to check his vitals and his blood work again. When the blood report came back they were astonished. Everything was normal, no bad blood count or tainted blood. The doctors and even the mother was baffled, befuddled and dumbfounded. She called me crying in disbelief, knowing God had performed a miracle. His wish to the "Make a Wish Foundation" was to go on a Disney cruise. I said to his mother, "Sure, go on the cruise, but he isn't dying. Instead, he shall live and see the goodness of the Lord in the land of the living."

As I did more altar calls I started running into the same problem; not having enough time to get some people completely free. In turn, I started doing deliverance at my house. By faith people were being set free, everything from wombs being opened to generational curses broken. One case in particular exposed my wife to the complete operation of hell and demons on earth. We later realized that over the years God was strategically preparing

38

us for warfare. This came with another experiential lesson that ultimately led to demons infiltrating my house.

Let's pray. God I thank you for Life, health and strength. I also thank you for your Word. Through John you said that your desire is for us "To prosper, be in good health, even as our soul prospers." God I thank you for prosperity in my mind, finances and health! Be glorified in my life! Let your perfect will be done. Amen

Notes

Chapter VI

Satan's Plan and Operation

In previous chapters, I explained my progression in deliverance. Starting with altar calls, ending with commanding demons to disclose pertinent information such as, their name, how they entered, when they entered, and ending with exorcism. At the time, I thought that was the totality of the process. What I didn't know would hurt me and haunt me for months.

I started conducting deliverance out of my home only for people I knew that were suffering or living in bondage. One afternoon I received a call from a family at my church. The parents had problems with their teenage daughter who recently finished high school. Let's call her Jane. They told me Jane was extremely paranoid and was possibly doing drugs. Since the family were long-standing members of the church, I set up a time to have them bring their daughter by. Jane was an active member of the church, very talented and outgoing. I figured a little counseling and prayer would be all she needed. When they were in route to my house I received a phone call from their car. I could hear Jane in the background screaming and moaning. Her mother was very frantic and unnerved saying over and over, "I don't know what to do!" I asked her to put Jane on the phone. She put the phone to Jane's mouth and Jane repeatedly screamed, "Something is wrong! Something is wrong!" A few minutes later they pulled up at my house. I went outside to meet them at the car. I opened the door and Jane started screaming saying, "They are in me!" "Demons are attacking me! I see them!" We got her in the house. I grabbed my anointing oil and Bible and began to pray. As I prayed, her eyes started rolling in her head and she was convulsing. The Lord spoke to my spirit and told me I would need help. Even though my wife assisted in other cases, I did not want her to be involved immediately in this situation. I knew this was a bad case of possession unlike I had ever seen before. I called a deacon from the church that stayed nearby and asked for assistance. Immediately, this trusted older gentlemen, my right hand guy at the church, came right over. For three hours straight we did deliverance. Four demons were cast out, the last one calling himself, "Hell." After Hell was cast out anticipating the manifestation of another demon, I continued to say, "Spirit what is your name?" Instead Jane said, "It's me, its Jane what happened?" Typically when deliverance is over, demons no longer submerge and suppress their victim allowing their innocence and personhood to emerge. We gave her a hug and started gasping in relief, thanking God it was over. My deacon went back to his house and we all decided to get something to eat and relax.

Two hours later she started having the same symptoms. I called and asked my deacon to come back over and this time for five hours straight we did deliverance. Let me pause parenthetically and say, as I speak about the operation of hell and demons I will purposely leave out some of the details of exorcism. I will say I have witnessed unbelievable body contortions. I've seen bodies completely elevate off the surface beneath them, objects disappear, and demons speak in multiple foreign languages, regurgitation of unexplainable matter, unbelievable acts of strength, disclosure of family names and demonic entry points dating back decades that proved to be true. Much of what I have experienced over the past decade is recorded. Also, on the website are testimonials and eyewitness accounts.

Someone may say well it shouldn't take all of that. I have heard pastors say if you have power and authority demons should come out immediately. Sometimes demons do come out immediately but in severe cases of possession when a person is overcome and indwelled by hundreds of spirits it is not an immediate process. For Example.

(Mark 9:21-29) [21] *"So He asked his father, "How long has this been happening to him?" And he said, "From childhood.* [22] *And often he has thrown him both into the fire and into the water to destroy him. But if you can do anything, have compassion on us and help us." [23] Jesus said to him, "If you can believe, all things are possible to him who believes." Immediately the father*

43

of the child cried out and said with tears, "Lord, I believe; help my unbelief!" When Jesus saw that the people came running together, He rebuked the unclean spirit, saying to it, "Deaf and dumb spirit, I command you, come out of him and enter him no more!" ²⁶ Then the spirit cried out, convulsed him greatly, and came out of him. And he became as one dead, so that many said, "He is dead." ²⁷ But Jesus took him by the hand and lifted him up, and he arose.

²⁸ And when He had come into the house, His disciples asked Him privately, "Why could we not cast it out?" ²⁹ So He said to them, "This kind can come out by nothing but prayer and fasting."

In this case, before the demon came out it did two things and we do not know for how long. The demon started screaming. Demonic screams are unlike any other and can last for minutes as the demons cry out in torture and frustration. Lastly, the spirit convulsed the boy. Imagine being tossed back and forth by a sumo wrestler over and over against your strength and will. The victim is left drained and exhausted such as the young boy here in the text. Then there is this story in scripture about the demon possessed man living in the tombs.

(Mark 5:2- 13) *"² And when He had come out of the boat, immediately there met Him out of the tombs a man with an unclean spirit, ³ who had his dwelling among the tombs; and no one could bind him,[b] not even with chains, ⁴ because he had often been bound with shackles and chains, and the chains had been pulled apart by him, and the shackles broken in pieces; neither could anyone tame him. ⁵ And always, night and day, he was in the mountains and in the tombs, crying out and cutting himself with stones.*

⁶ When he saw Jesus from afar, he ran and worshiped Him. ⁷ And he cried out with a loud voice and said, "What have I to do with You, Jesus, Son of the Most High God? I implore you by God that you do not torment me."

44

⁸ For He said to him, "Come out of the man, unclean spirit!"
⁹ Then He asked him, "What is your name?" And he answered, saying, "My name is Legion; for we are many." ¹⁰ Also he begged Him earnestly that He would not send them out of the country.

¹¹ Now a large herd of swine was feeding there near the mountains. ¹² So all the demons begged Him, saying, "Send us to the swine, that we may enter them." ¹³ And at once Jesus[c] gave them permission. Then the unclean spirits went out and entered the swine (there were about two thousand); and the herd ran violently down the steep place into the sea, and drowned in the sea."

In this case, the man had enough demons in him to fill up a herd of pigs numbering 2,000! My point is, you can never determine how long a deliverance session should take or know exactly how many demons may be indwelling in someone possessed. I also learned through study and my experience that demons operate in family groupings. In the family there is hierarchy. At the head of each family is a strongman. The strongman is the first demon in the family to gain access. This demon then provides an access point for weaker demons to enter. Amongst demons that rule families there is rank, such as generals, queens, kings, and witches that rank even above strongholds. Ultimately, the highest rank belongs to Satan himself. Likewise, just as demons rank and operate in order, they also come out in order. A strongman or a ruling spirit will never come out first. Most of his or her strength is garnered from weaker spirits that come in after them. For example, if the strongman is anger, confusion or depression, these are some of the demons I've witnessed come out of those families.

Strongman of Anger:

Frustration, wrath, hatred, rage, resentment, temper, bitterness tantrums, spoiled.

Strongman of Confusion: Indecision, lack of focus, ADD

(Attention Deficit Disorder), ADHD (Attention Deficit Hyperactivity Disorder), OCD (Obsessive Compulsive Disorder), disconnect, deception.

Strongman of Depression: Discouragement, despair, hopelessness, despondent, self-pity, tired, insomnia, suicide, withdrawal, loneliness, victim.

Keep in mind these are just three among dozens of strongholds that can infiltrate one person. Again in cases such as this, the process of exorcism can take weeks even months to get someone completely free. In the case at hand, the only reason I was able to go hours was because of love and the power of God that strengthened me throughout the process. After five hours of deliverance, the last spirit to come out was Lucifer. It was then that peace entered the room, the young lady returned to normalcy and the exorcism process was over.

A few months passed and I received another call (same girl, same situation). When she arrived at the house her condition was worse. Her physical condition and appearance had changed drastically due to the attack on her body. I informed my wife that this time I would not call anybody over and we would conduct deliverance. What was happening did not make sense to me. For some reason this young lady had a portal that gave demons direct access to her life! I began to ask a series of questions about her upbringing, grandparents, siblings and I finally asked her had she ever called or visited a psychic. To that last question she responded, yes.

Let's pray. God your Word declares, "God hath not given us the spirit of fear, but of power and of love and of a sound mind." You have also given me authority to overcome and pull down strongholds. I thank you for your son that died on the cross for my sins and rose with all power. You said in Romans 8:11 *"But if the Spirit of Him who raised Jesus from the dead dwells in you, He who raised Christ Jesus from the dead will also give*

life to your mortal bodies through His Spirit who indwells you."
I thank you that I am victorious and can do all things through Christ who strengthens me.

Notes

Chapter VII

The Danger of Psychics

The Bible speaks strongly against the use of clairvoyants, psychics, horoscopes, tarot cards, Ouija boards or any other aspect of the occult. In
The Old Testament, mediums were common among the pagans and God warned the children of Israel against becoming involved in these practices just prior to their entry into the Promised Land of Canaan.

(Deuteronomy 18:10-12) "When you come into the land which the Lord your God is giving you, you shall not learn to follow the abominations of those nations. [10] There shall not be found among you anyone who makes his son or his daughter pass through the fire, or one who practices witchcraft, or a soothsayer, or one who interprets omens, or a sorcerer, [11] or one who conjures spells, or a medium, or a spiritualist, or one who calls up the dead. [12] For all who do these things are an abomination to the Lord, and because of these abominations the Lord your God drives them out from before you."

In the New Testament there is also a compelling story showing Godly disdain for fortune telling.

(Acts 16:16-19) [16] Now it happened, as we went to prayer, that a certain slave girl possessed with a spirit of divination met us, who brought her masters much profit by fortune-telling. [17] This girl followed Paul and us, and cried out, saying, "These men are the servants of the Most High God, who proclaim to us the way of salvation." [18] And this she did for many days. But Paul, greatly annoyed, turned and said to the spirit, "I command you in the name of Jesus Christ to come out of her." And he came out that very hour. [19] But when her masters saw that their hope of profit was gone, they seized Paul and Silas and dragged them into the marketplace to the authorities."

50

These scriptures inform us that psychics receive their power from Satan and demonic forces. Check out this blog from "Beyond Today."

"Familiar spirits, in reality disguised demons, *can* have an intimate knowledge of people, alive or dead. They have at their disposal an extensive network of information from fellow demons that are more than willing to share their knowledge with the deceived "host." In this way, they will entice many more people to be deceived and hooked ending sometimes as pawns to these spirits. This is the grave danger of participating in any of these practices.

At first these spirits appear as willing servants, but inevitably they end up as harsh taskmasters. That is why we should avoid coming into *any* contact with people who claim they can communicate with the dead. God, who is intimately familiar with this spirit world, warns us that the person who turns to mediums and familiar spirits, to prostitute himself with them, *I will set my face against that person and cut him off from his people" (Leviticus 20:6).*

Needless to say, when Jane informed us she went to a psychic with some friends, I understood the magnitude of the task before us. During my first year in ministry, I had an encounter with another female in her early 40's who visited a psychic. To say the least, I failed miserably in my efforts to deliver her. Back then I was enthusiastic, on fire, and untrained, still finding my way in the area of deliverance. I was asked by a relative to please visit with their friend who was sickly. When we arrived we all sat down in the living room and she began to tell me about her problems. Everything in her life was under attack: finances, children, relationship, job and her health. I knew enough to know that demons were responsible for the destruction. She then pulled up her shirt and stated she had some type of outward tumor or hernia that kept appearing on her stomach. Well, bless God whatever it was, it decided to appear while we were there. In my head I said to myself, "What's really going on here?" I said to her, "You are under attack and there is something in this house that's not right." The truth is, I really wasn't excited about finding out what it was. We started walking through the house and I started looking under books and moving objects out of the way basically looking for some form of demonic paraphernalia. She stated, "I have a rabbit's foot under my bed and a few other things." I asked her where she got it. She said it was given to her by a psychic with some other things she needed to put under her pillow. She began to express how this psychic requested pertinent personal information about her and her children and how she was given things to put under her and her children's pillows. I knew the purpose of that demand was to give demons access to her and her household. We went back downstairs and I said "We need to pray." We all held hands in a circle. I prayed and prayed and prayed and prayed. I prayed soft, I prayed loud, quoted scripture, spoke in tongues and literally nothing. I mean nothing happened. When I was done she looked at me, gave me a hug and said thank you.

Listen pastors, preachers, evangelist. When you are dealing with demonic forces on this level your religious prayer will not work. You will need more than a few memorized scriptures and traditional church quotes to defeat these demons. In the next Chapter "Your Religious Prayer Won't Work," you'll read about how I encountered demons that spoke more tongues and quoted more scripture than my whole church combined. When we left the house I hoped for the best and never returned. Even though I did not get the results I wanted, the experience helped to prepare me for what was before me.

Let's Pray! God help me to develop an authentic relationship with you. God I do not want religion. I want you, your power, glory and wisdom. As the deer pants for the water brooks, so my soul pants for You, O God.

Notes

Chapter VIII

Your Religious Prayer Won't Work

I remember one day when Ivy and I were preparing to have a function at our house. We had several families coming and we were rushing to get the house together. With many things to do, I decided to get vacuuming out of the way. I cut the vacuum on and was expeditiously going from one room to the next. When reaching the third room I realized the vacuum wasn't picking up. The motor was running but accomplishing nothing. I was simply going through the motions. Often times when we pray that is exactly what we are doing, just going through the motions. The motor is running but nothing is being accomplished. When I prayed for the lady in the previous chapter my motor was running but nothing was accomplished.

There was a minister at my first church that could pray the house down. Oh, the members loved to hear him pray. His prayer was like a traditional hymn, sermon and poem all mashed together into one 15 minute exhortation. By the time he finished people were shouting and crying. They would say "Boy, that man knows he can pray!" Truth be told, I liked hearing him pray too, even though it was the same prayer over and over. We knew how it would start, what was in the middle and how it would end. I'm telling you that in one prayer, he would take us all the way down to hell and the grave then back up to Heaven! It sounded good, felt good, but for the most part it was no good! It was a high we became dependent on which temporarily anesthetized our pain but lacked power to destroy the yokes of bondage.

(Matthew 6:7-8) "And when you pray, do not use vain repetitions as the heathen do. For they think that they will be heard for their many words."

Many in the church have become satisfied with having a form of Godliness. We are preaching, singing, dancing, and praying. Is it talent or anointing, performance or worship, a job or service? Albeit you may not know the difference, but heaven and hell does. If your gift and what you do for the church is not reflective in your lifestyle, what you think you're doing for Christ may actually bring more glory to the devil. Remember, demons like to perform. It doesn't matter if it's a liturgical dance, worship leading or gospel rapping. When the experience is over if people are clapping for you and not for the God who used you, the enemy has won! Child of God, there must be power through relationship attached to your gift. Let's look at this passage.

(Luke 10:1-10, 17-19) *"After these things the Lord appointed seventy others also, and sent them two by two before His face into every city and place where He Himself was about to go. [2] Then He said to them, "The harvest truly is great, but the laborers are few; therefore pray the Lord of the harvest to send out laborers into His harvest. [3] Go your way; behold, I send you out as lambs among wolves. [4] Carry neither money bag, knapsack, nor sandals; and greet no one along the road. [5] But whatever house you enter, first say, 'Peace to this house.' [6] And if a son of peace is there, your peace will rest on it; if not, it will return to you. [7] And remain in the same house, eating and drinking such things as they give, for the laborer is worthy of his wages. Do not go from house to house. [8] Whatever city you enter, and they receive you, eat such things as are set before you. [9] And heal the sick there, and say to them, 'The kingdom of God has come near to you.' [10] But whatever city you enter, and they do not receive you, go out into its streets and say, [11] 'The very dust of your city which clings to us we wipe off against you. Nevertheless know this that the kingdom of God has come near you.' [12] But I say to you that it will be more tolerable in that Day for Sodom than for that city."*

[17] "Then the seventy returned with joy, saying, "Lord, even the demons are subject to us in your name." [18] And He said to them,

"I saw Satan fall like lightning from heaven. [19] Behold, I give you the authority to trample on serpents and scorpions, and over all the power of the enemy, and nothing shall by any means hurt you.)

In this passage Jesus gave the seventy temporary power and authority to go throughout the land healing and spreading the gospel. When they got back, in Verse 17, some realized they had power over demons. Acts 2 discloses what was temporary became permanent.

(Acts 2) "When the Day of Pentecost had fully come, they were all with one accord in one place. [2] And suddenly there came a sound from heaven, as of a rushing mighty wind, and it filled the whole house where they were sitting. [3] Then there appeared to them divided tongues, as of fire, and one sat upon each of them. [4] And they were all filled with the Holy Spirit and began to speak with other tongues, as the Spirit gave them utterance."

(Romans 8:11) states [11] But if the Spirit of Him who raised Jesus from the dead dwells in you, He who raised Christ from the dead will also give life to your mortal bodies through His Spirit who dwells in you."

In other words, if you are saved, the spirit of power, the mighty rushing wind is in you. It's there but you must be filled with it. One evidence of this power and filling is the gift of tongues. Now if you cannot speak in tongues it does not mean you are not saved or you lack an authentic relationship with Christ. It just means you have a slight power shortage. For example, my vehicle has eight spark plugs. It can very well run off seven but for optimum performance all eight are needed. Listen to what Paul says about tongues.

(I Corinthians 14:1-3, 14-15) *"Pursue love, and desire spiritual gifts, but especially that you may prophesy.* [2] *For he who speaks in a tongue does not speak to men but to God, for no one understands him; however, in the spirit he speaks mysteries.* [14] *For if I pray in a tongue, my spirit prays, but my understanding is unfruitful.* [15] *What is the conclusion then? I will pray with the spirit, and I will also pray with the understanding. I will sing with the spirit, and I will also sing with the understanding."*

He first classifies tongues as a gift all can have if so desired but the point I want to make is he states clearly that you are speaking to God in a spiritual language that Heaven understands. I can't explain the mystery but I do know when I have prayed in the spirit during deliverance, demons have cried out, cursed me out and come out! Now when praying publicly it's not necessary to pray in tongues to display power. The power of your prayer comes from your connection to the Father. When Jesus was on earth the Bible said many times he prayed all night long and often withdrew into the wilderness to pray. Now if Jesus had to spend time with God and pray to get power how much more should we? Many have good religion but your power will come from your relationship with Christ.

(Ephesians 3:20) *"Now unto him that is able to do exceeding abundantly above all that we ask or think, according to the power that worketh in us,"*

Do you have a relationship with God that produces power or are you just going through the religious motions? Demons know the difference. Remember again what the demon said to the man that had a form of Godliness seeking to operate in power he did not possess. The evil spirit answered and said, "Jesus

59

I know, and Paul I know; but who are you? Then the man in whom the evil spirit was leaped on them, overpowered them, and prevailed against them, so that they fled out of that house naked and wounded."

There is a day coming when the authenticity of your relationship with Christ will be tested such as mine was in this next chapter.

Let's Pray: God forgive me for putting situations, things and people in front of my relationship with you. God I don't want religion. I desire a true relationship with you. Holy Spirit help me to stay connected to the power source. I am nothing without you God. As the song says, "Lead me, guide me along the way, Lord if you lead me I will not stray. Lord let me walk each day with thee, lead me Oh Lord lead me."

Notes

Chapter IX

Ready for War

When Jane expressed to me and Ivy that she visited a psychic, I mentally started to prepare and pray. The parents considered taking the girl to the hospital. I responded by saying if you do so in the condition she is in, they are going to deem her suicidal or mentally unstable and capable of hurting herself. She could then very easily wind up in a psychiatric ward. We asked the parents to let Jane stay with us for a while, giving us time to nourish her physically, spiritually and mentally. This was a very serious situation but Ivy and I had already gone through a lot. Together we stared death and hell in the face. Therefore, we knew what we were dealing with and understood that God wanted to use us to save this young girl's life.

After we all spoke for a while there seemed to be a sense of relief and optimism. The parents left and we talked to Jane about her future and the Will of God for her life before we all went to sleep. The next morning Ivy went to check on Jane. She was squirming with stomach pain saying she had been up all night long. Ivy came and got me and I immediately started to pray over Jane's stomach. Within minutes a demonic spirit manifested. We went through the same process spoken of in prior chapters demanding a name. When I laid my hand on her stomach the demonic spirit spoke and in a deep moan said, "Pain." I said, "Look at me and say it again!" When doing deliverance eye contact is extremely important. Demons sense fear and look for it! The eyes are the window to the soul and when demons see intensity and the fire of the Holy Ghost burning in your eyes they cower and respond.

Gritting her teeth the spirit growled and hollered, "Pain!" The tone of this demon was eerie and aggressive. I then asked, "How did you gain access?" The demon said through "Hurt." Hurt was actually another demon (remember demons work in family groupings). I then asked, "How long have you been in her?" Pain responded saying, "four years." I then said, "In the name of Jesus come out!" She convulsed, her eyes rolled up in her head and she turned over. I said, "Look at me and speak your name?" Hurt manifested. This demon immediately started cussing and flailing Jane's hands as if she were fighting. I stood back while Ivy prayed and watched as the demon caused Jane to cry and fight the air as if someone was there. Then in an authoritative voice, I said, "I take authority over you. In the name of Jesus sit down!" I laid my hands on her head and commanded Hurt to leave. When Hurt left another spirit started to manifest. I said, "Look at me, what is your name? The demon said, "Rock!" We later learned that Rock was an ex-boyfriend who had mistreated her and was verbally abusive. This is how Hurt and Pain entered. Many more demons came out and that particular deliverance session lasted three hours. At the end of Jane's first week at our house, she was delivered from nearly 50 demons. Ivy and I could not believe what we witnessed with our own eyes. We were up the majority of the week all night long. This was a pattern I was familiar with; going to sleep around 3AM and waking up at 6AM to get the kids to school. I knew God kept me and his strength was made perfect in my weakness.

For about two weeks things were calm. We thought Jane was finally free. Jane asked did we mind if she spent some time with some friends who were in town. We did not want to keep her in bondage at our home but she was temporarily in our custody. We decided to sit Jane down and remind her of all she had been delivered from. We specifically told her that smoking, drinking and lasciviousness were all portals for demons to gain access to her life.

Jane hung out with her friends and the next day everything

seemed to be fine. About 1AM, we heard a knock on our bedr
door. It was Jane. Not wanting to wake the kids, we told hᴗ.
come in and shut the door. She walked in crying, bent over in
pain. We got up. Ivy told her to lie across our bed. At this point
the demons knew deliverance was about to occur. Immediately
she started moaning and turning. As I often would, with my
phone or computer, I'd log on to YouTube and play a worship
song very popular in the church. I can't express how important
it is to set the atmosphere for deliverance. Music can help in
driving out evil spirits.

*(I Samuel 16:22-23) "Then Saul sent to Jesse, saying,
"Please let David stand before me, for he has found favor in my
sight." ²³ And so it was, whenever the spirit from God was upon
Saul, that David would take a harp and play it with his hand.
Then Saul would become refreshed and well, and the distressing
spirit would depart from him."*

In this particular situation the demon began to mock the
song singing along with the music. The spirit then started taunting
me. After realizing I was not moved, it directed its attention
towards Ivy. This demon on all four's crawled slowly to the end
of the bed where Ivy was sitting and cursed her out doing all it
could to make Ivy feel fear and guilt. Ivy matched the intensity
of the spirit and rebuked it. The demon started laughing but left
her alone. I decided just to step back and watch just to see what
this spirit would do. When the song went off this demon stood
up in the bed as if it were holding a microphone and continued
singing other church choir songs. This demonic spirit sung three
songs. I can't remember all the songs but I know one of the three
was, "This Little Light of Mine." She sung for like five minutes
straight, real loud and angry in a broken demonic tone as if the
demon sang under duress.

After the demon finished performing, it started clapping Jane's hands looking at us saying, "Clap for me M*****F*****." We could not laugh out loud but inside Ivy and I thought it was absolutely hilarious that this demon was literally mad because we would not clap. The spirit stood on the bed and started to spin the ceiling fan and all of a sudden the lights in the room started flickering. As dust fell from the fan blades this demon started to say, "The dust of hell." I immediately cleaned the fan blades (We learned through other experiences demonic spirits seek to dwell in uncleanliness.) I decided it was time to take authority over the situation. The problem was I had given this spirit too much of a platform. The next few hours were exhausting but God showed up.

When I finished cleaning the fan blades there was dust in the air. This demon stood back up, raised Jane's hands and began to waive the dust towards Jane's mouth as if the dust was giving it power. I asked Ivy to leave the room and pray knowing these demons would sometimes attack her. I then grabbed my anointing oil and said, "In the name of Jesus I take authority over you!" I pulled Jane down to the bed and the demon then started trying to take the oil out of my hand. At this point I was literally in a wrestling match with a demon. I pushed the demon completely off me. The demon cocked Jane's fist back as if it was going to try to punch me. For the next 30 seconds we stared eye to eye. (Please understand the eyes are the gateway to the soul and demons seek to detect fear. If fear is detected the fear becomes an inlet for paranoia and worry.) This demon could sense no fear in me, but I could not let anger take over either. I had to gain my composure quickly and fight spiritually. I unleashed scripture after scripture starting with, "No weapon formed against me shall prosper" speaking in tongues in between. Tongues or praying in the spirit is an important part of the process.

Again, this demon hoped I would succumb to anger and physically harm Jane, empowering the demon to later use it against me. At the foot of the bed was some type of fabric cord for a dress. The demon grabbed the cord, put it around Jane's neck and made her choke herself. Ivy came back in and could not believe what she was witnessing. As soon as I got the cord out of her hand, the demon took control of Jane's hands, grabbed her neck and started choking her saying, "I am going to kill this b****. I am going to kill her! She knows too much! She must die!"

After I got her hands from around her neck the Holy Spirit directed me to do something completely out of the norm. I asked Ivy to get me a bottle of water. I quickly prayed over the bottle and anointed it. When Ivy left out again, I stood back and began to thrust the water with my fingers tips into Jane's face saying, "Fire from the Holy Ghost!" The spirit was being tormented and started crying and saying, "Stop! It burns! It burns!" After doing this for about 10 minutes I put my hand on Jane's head and said, "Demon what is your name?" In a menacing diabolical tone the demon looked me dead in the eyes and said, "Devil!" I said, "Say it again louder!" It said again, "Devil, you fool!" I started praying in the spirit and suddenly I could feel the presence of God in the room. I continued speaking in tongues and saying God I feel your presence! I dropped down to my knees and lay prostrate on the floor and began to cry. I felt angels and the presence of Christ in the room. The demon and every diabolical force around it was paralyzed as the presence and power of God invaded the room. For five minutes I could not lift my head or body off the floor. My body was paralyzed in a posture of worship! All I could do was cry and give God glory!

(II Chronicles 5:13-14) "It came even to pass, as the

trumpeters and singers were as one, to make one sound to be heard in praising and thanking the Lord; and when they lifted up their voice with the trumpets and cymbals and instruments of music, and praised the Lord, saying, For he is good; for his mercy endures forever: that then the house was filled with a cloud, even the house of the Lord; [14] So that the priests could not stand to minister by reason of the cloud: for the glory of the Lord had filled the house of God."

This passage of scripture describes a worship service and how when the glory of God showed up the priest had to fall down and worship. This experience forever changed me. I only shared it with Ivy knowing she would believe me predicated upon other experiences and how the power of God worked through me to heal and deliver. I wish every believer could experience the manifest presence of God. It would eliminate any doubt about Heaven, its glory and the power of God!

When I got off the floor the demon was still on the bed on all fours. It looked up at me with a look I had not seen before; a look of trepidation and befuddlement. The devil spoke softly with a question, "Who are you? Who are you?" For me, outside of what was just experienced with God's glory filling the room, it was an empowering moment. It told me this demon may have thought it knew me predicated upon my past and former weaknesses. But what happened in that room made the devil change his mind about who he was contending with. Beloved, your past does not define you; rather, it prepares! Don't allow the enemy to make you believe you're not worthy or you have done too much to be justified and loved. Please take in these words from one of my favorite chapters in the Bible.

(Romans 8:28-39) [28] And we know that all things work

together for good to those who love God, to those who are the called according to His purpose. [29] For whom He foreknew, He also predestined to be conformed to the image of His Son, that He might be the firstborn among many brethren. [30] Moreover whom He predestined, these He also called; whom He called, these He also justified; and whom He justified, these He also glorified. [31] What then shall we say to these things? If God is for us, who can be against us? [32] He who did not spare His own Son, but delivered Him up for us all, how shall He not with Him also freely give us all things? [33] Who shall bring a charge against God's elect? It is God who justifies. [34] Who is he who condemns? It is Christ who died, and furthermore is also risen, who is even at the right hand of God, who also makes intercession for us. [35] Who shall separate us from the love of Christ? Shall tribulation, or distress, or persecution, or famine, or nakedness, or peril, or sword? [36] As it is written, "For Your sake we are killed all day long; We are accounted as sheep for the slaughter." [37] Yet in all these things we are more than conquerors through Him who loved us. [38] For I am persuaded that neither death nor life, nor angels nor principalities nor powers, nor things present nor things to come, [39] nor height nor depth, nor any other created thing, shall be able to separate us from the love of God which is in Christ Jesus our Lord."

If you just read that, right about now you should feel invincible and full of confidence knowing God had your back, has your back, and will have your back. As a result you can't back down! The enemy of your soul is defeated.

(Colossians 1:21-22)   " [21] And you, who once were alienated and enemies in your mind by wicked works, yet now He has reconciled [22] in the body of His flesh through death, to present you holy, and blameless, and above reproach in His sight."

Having these scriptures buried in my heart, I responded to the devils' question by saying, "I am a child of the King, heir of salvation, a warrior for Christ redeemed by the blood! Now in the name of Christ the Son of the Living God, I command you to leave this body!" The demon immediately came out! Hallelujah! Hallelujah! Hallelujah! After this, as usual, Jane returned to herself. She asked, "What happened? What's going on? I feel so much better!" She then began to cry uncontrollably knowing God was with her, sustaining her and keeping her through it all. As I mentioned earlier, through this experience I also learned demons like to perform and there is a difference between performing and worship. Remember Satan was kicked out of heaven because he desired to be exalted and worshipped above God.

(Isaiah 14:11-14) *"Your pomp is brought down to Sheol, And the sound of your stringed instruments; The maggot is spread under you,*
And worms cover you. "12 "How you are fallen from heaven, O Lucifer,[a] son of the morning! How you are cut down to the ground, You who weakened the nations! 13 For you have said in your heart; 'I will ascend into heaven, I will exalt my throne above the stars of God; I will also sit on the mount of the congregation on the farthest sides of the north;
14 I will ascend above the heights of the clouds,
I will be like the Most High. "

Some singers sing to be glorified and others sing to create glory for God. The need to be acknowledged and praised as seen in this scripture is a spirit from hell that takes over many worship services, putting the worship leader or even the pastor in the place of God. As mentioned, the devil stopped singing and was frustrated because we didn't clap. If you need a crowd to preach, music to sing, or people to approve you to validate your worship, you may need to ask yourself, "Is Jesus really the center of my joy? Is this about Him or is it about me and my ego?" I personally have learned the difference between the two. When ministry is about you it makes you arrogant. When your ministry and service is unto God remembering where you came from, still wondering why He saved you, you walk in humility and patience exalting others above yourself.

Let's pray: Lord draw me closer to thee. If there is anything in me that is unlike you, that's hindering my worship or blocking my blessings, God please remove it. Or as David prayed in *Psalms 51:10-13* *"¹⁰ Create in me a clean heart, O God; and renew a right spirit within me.¹¹ Cast me not away from thy presence; and take not thy holy spirit from me.¹² Restore unto me the joy of thy salvation; and uphold me with thy free spirit.¹³ Then will I teach transgressors thy ways; and sinners shall be converted unto thee."* God I bless you for sacrificing your Son and raising Him up! Victory in Jesus my Savior forever! Amen.

Notes

Chapter X

Fighting With the Devil

After having expelled well over a hundred demonic spirits, with the last one declaring himself to be the devil, I assumed the process had finally come to an end. Everything was going well and Jane once again seemed to be normal. The entire week she smiled, praised God and read her Word. That Saturday, we talked about some of the miraculous things we witnessed God do over the months. At one point, we all looked at each other and chuckled saying, "You know we can't share this with anyone. People will think we have lost it." We laughed and talked for a couple of hours then I remember specifically Jane going to my daughter's room and giving her a kiss goodnight. At the time, I couldn't figure out why, but it really concerned me. I did not say anything; instead, I later went into the room and prayed over my 2 1/2 year old little girl. Afterwards, we all eventually went to bed anticipating church the next day.

Sunday morning at about 8AM, Ivy went into Jane's room just to talk and get ready for church. About thirty minutes later I heard a lot of fussing and yelling. I proceeded into the room noticing Ivy was extremely upset. Ivy, because of her own battle, became very discerning, sensing when Jane wasn't quite right and in need of prayer. When Ivy went into the room, she felt that Jane's behavior was a little erratic. As a result, she told Jane, "I believe you should let Mark pray with you." Jane said, "I'm fine, I don't need prayer. Ivy insisted and when I came in Jane was a bit irate saying, "I'm tired of doing this, I'm fine, I'm going home, all of this is stupid." I said to Jane, "It's all good, let's just settle down and get ready for church." Jane replied by saying, "I am not going to church!" At this point I was in disbelief thinking this can't be another demon. Ivy and I went back to our room and by this time the kids were up. I said to Ivy, "Maybe she is really just tired." Ivy said, "No she needs prayer! Are you going to pray with her?" We went back and forth and she won. I went back in the room. "Jane, how do you feel?" I asked. Upset she stated "I am fine!" I said, "Well let's go to church." She said, "No I don't feel like going to stupid church!" At this point I realized Ivy was right and Jane needed deliverance. I did not want to start deliverance because I knew this demon wanted to rattle me with confrontation and I really needed to get to church. I had grown accustomed to Sunday confrontations, sometimes getting to church just in time to preach. So I said, "You must be tired Jane, go ahead stay here and get some rest, we love you, and maybe you don't need to go to church today."

When demons are operating through people they want to argue. What I find to be most difficult is the fact that they have the ability to make their victim believe the ones who love them are against them. Therefore, loved ones and close friends with their best interest at hand, demons will drive away through confrontation. Demons thrive in conflict, fighting and confusion. Overtime, I have really learned to embrace the scriptures below. These scriptures have literally changed my position, life, and when applied correctly given me the upper hand in dealing with demons such as in this situation with Jane.

(Ephesians 6:12) *"For we do not wrestle against flesh and blood, but against principalities, against powers, against the rulers of the darkness of this age, against spiritual hosts of wickedness in the heavenly places."*

In this passage Paul specifically tells us that our fight is not with flesh and blood meaning our fight is never with people but demons that work through people to attack us and destroy relationships.

(Proverbs 15) *"A soft answer turns away wrath, but a*

harsh word stirs up anger."

(I Peter 3:8-9) "Finally, all of you be of one mind, having compassion for one another; love as brothers, be tenderhearted, be courteous; ⁹ not returning evil for evil or reviling for reviling, but on the contrary blessing, knowing that you were called to this, that you may inherit a blessing."

Peter tells us in this passage to be tender hearted not returning evil for evil or cussing for cussing, but do the opposite. The devil's job is to get both parties involved heated, frustrated, and contentious with the ultimate goal of physical conflict. You can't fight fire with fire. Someone must use water! For example, Jane did need to be in church but I knew the demon wanted to make going to church a source of contention. Through the wisdom of the Holy Ghost I spoke in love, agreed with the demon, extinguishing the fire with the water of the Word. Loving Jane through her uncontrollable temper left the demonic spirit speechless.

We went to church praying Jane would be there when we returned. When we arrived home, Jane was lying on the couch in the living room groaning diabolically having severe pain attacks in her stomach. I told Ivy to leave and take the kids out for a few hours. Just getting home from church, I was drained, my clothes were wet, and all I really wanted to do was take a shower, eat, and watch the game. At that moment I was captured by love and hate at the same time. We loved this girl, knew her future was bright and that God had a plan for her life. At the same time after having gone through so many deliverance sessions, I had great disdain for demons, how they operate, their purpose, their master and what they do to their victims.

76

This deliverance session plays in my head like a movie. I took my jacket off and set up the computer to play the same worship song I spoke about in previous chapters all the while praying in the spirit. However, this time I did not have to demand that the spirit reveal its name. Smirking and laughing the spirit sat up on the couch and said, "I'mmmm baaack. It's the devil you fool!" I asked, "How did you regain access to this body?" The demon responded saying, "I never left, you f******f***!" In essence, even though the spirit left her, the spirit never left the atmosphere and before the week was out reentered her body lying dormant.

I cut the song on from YouTube on the computer and continued praying in an effort to charge the atmosphere with praise and power. I was inviting heaven in to take over the room. What the demon did next blew me away. Again, the demon started singing this song and the melody mocking the lyrics. The demon then looked at me and stated, "Don't you know I gave that whore her power?" Then without seeing the computer began to describe what the woman had on, and who was doing the cover for the hit worship song playing on the YouTube video! "She is a whore!" "I gave her power!" "I gave her the ability to sing!"

I couldn't believe it. I specifically chose this version of the song because it was powerful. It showed me how God will use people in spite of their imperfections, not allowing his word to return void. At the same time the enemy will work overtime to destroy that very individual's character. So the three inevitable results are: 1) People that don't know the artist will just respect and honor the anointing on their life. 2) Some that know their flaws will condemn them as hypocrites and will not follow or listen. 3) Lastly, some will respect the gift God has placed in them and continue to support the artist separating the anointing and gift from the flawed individual.

Even though the devil declared to have given this person their power to sing, I did not turn the music off. Instead, I started singing the song. I told the enemy whoever is singing does not affect the power of God's Word or name. I then quoted Isaiah 55:8-11.

"For My thoughts are not your thoughts,
Nor are your ways My ways," says the Lord.
⁹ "For as the heavens are higher than the earth,
So are My ways higher than your ways, and My thoughts than your thoughts. ¹⁰ "For as the rain comes down, and the snow from heaven, and do not return there, But water the earth, and make it bring forth and bud that it may give seed to the sower and bread to the eater, ¹¹ So shall My word be that goes forth from My mouth; It shall not return to Me void, But it shall accomplish what I please, And it shall prosper in the thing for which I sent it."

I say again, "His Word cannot and will not return void!" The devil was extremely irritated. He started to make Jane pound her head on the arm rest of the couch. I put my hand on her forehead and stated, "I take authority over you in the name of Jesus!" Immediately, the spirit stopped convulsing her. Then, grabbing my forearm with both hands, the spirit wanted to sink her fingernails into my skin and claw me with all of its might. It was literally squeezing the air unable to penetrate as if an invisible power was between her nails and my skin. The demon said, "I'm going to kill you! I am going to kill you! Get away! You stupid fool!"

The demon rolled off the couch and started squirming on the floor. I went through the same deliverance process spoken of earlier even using water. After nearly three hours of quoting scripture, praying in the spirit, thrusting water and commanding the devil to leave, the demon looked at me and said, "Where do I go? I responded saying, "To hell! Angels drag this demon to hell!" There was a loud scream then Jane's body fell flat to the floor. I started praying, "God restore and renew her!" Then as usual she came to herself asking what happened and why was she all wet? Simultaneously, Ivy was walking through the door with the children. God knew the exact moment they needed to walk through the door. There was no doubt in my mind that Jane was free from the spirit of the devil. What concerned me was the question the devil asked. "Where do I go?" By this time I had done many deliverances but I was not consistent in commanding the demons to return to hell. This question proposed by the spirit of the devil helped me to understand what gave the demon reaccess into her body. It never left the house! Concerned, I started wondering how many other demons were still in the atmosphere.

Let's pray. God, you are awesome! You sit high and look low. Just as the earth is beneath your feet, I thank you that the devil is beneath mine! Amen

Notes

Chapter XI

Demons in My House

(Matthew 12:43-45) "When an unclean spirit goes out of a man, he goes through dry places, seeking rest, and finds none. [44] Then he says, 'I will return to my house from which I came.' And when he comes, he finds it empty, swept, and put in order. [45] Then he goes and takes with him seven other spirits more wicked than himself, and they enter and dwell there; and the last state of that man is worse than the first. So shall it also be with this wicked generation."

This scripture describes exactly what we were experiencing in our house. I found that when demons are cast out without directive, they will attach themselves to anything in the house that's diabolical or evil: paintings, pictures, statues, figurines, books, jewelry, toys, stuffed animals, clothing, furniture, filth, etc. After delivering Jane from the spirit of the devil, I hoped it was over but I almost became numb to the process. By this time I had been doing deliverance more often than not for nearly two years. It had become a lifestyle. Every day I asked God when this would end. "God, this is taking time away from my family and church." My faith was in Romans 8:28, *"And we know all things work together for the good of them that love the Lord, and are the called according to his purpose."*

I knew I was called and that I loved the Lord, so I had to trust that His Word would come to pass. Still at times I felt like I was doing deliverance yet in bondage myself. My dilemma was, I couldn't just walk away and let the enemy win. Too many lives were at stake. For some strange reason God wanted me to understand the underworld. His will was for me to experience and witness Satan's operation on earth. Many have written books and given testimonials about going to hell. My case is somewhat different. I was never transported to hell; rather, hell was transported to my house.

After delivering Jane from the spirit of the devil for two weeks straight she had no issues. However, strange things started to happen in our home. One night my four year old son woke up in the middle of the night screaming, "Mommy! Mommy! We both ran to the room asking what was wrong. He said something was flying around in his room. I figured maybe he was having a bad dream so we prayed and waited in his room until he went back to sleep. The next night he woke up again this time saying, "Daddy!" I immediately jumped out of the bed and ran in the room. He said, "I saw something walking on the ceiling." I started thinking kids don't fake this stuff especially when they are trying to sleep. I got my anointing oil, anointed the ceiling and his walls and found a lamp to put in his room. Keeping the lamp light on helped him to sleep but I knew something was wrong and what he was seeing was real.

A few days later, when it came time to put my daughter to bed she became extremely restless. We never had any issues with her going to bed in her room and sleeping throughout the night. But again this night was different. We put her in her bed as usual and within minutes she started to cry and complain about her covers, then her pillow, then she wanted to change shirts. She said she was itching, hungry and not hungry. I got frustrated and demanded that she go to sleep and I left the room. She cried and cried. I figured she would eventually cry herself to sleep. Forty-five minutes passed and she was still crying. I went and got her, and brought her into our room. I never allowed the kids to sleep in the bed with us but this night we made an exception. The next night it was the same thing again but this time worse. When it was time to go to her room, she started rolling on the floor, crawling around and laughing. When I demanded that she get in bed and go to sleep again she cried and was very irritable.

That night I rocked her in my arms and prayed for close to 45 minutes until she fell asleep. This irritation continued and every night the cycle repeated itself with me having to spend upwards of 90 minutes rocking and lying next to my daughter in her bed for her to go to sleep.

A few weeks later Jane once again woke up in the middle of the night and knocked on our door. She did not look well. Nauseated and sweaty, she stated, "I am so sick." I am thinking in my head here we go again. I can't believe this is still happening. I assumed the process would be as usual with the same results. This time was unlike any other. I knew the anointing on my life was heavier because this time I immediately commanded the demon to speak and declare its name. After the third command the demon in a low menacing tone sounding like an old witch said, "Sorcerer." On her knees with her hands in the air and her hips moving in a circular motion, she stated again, "Sorcerer, Sorcerer, Sorcerer." I said, "How did you gain access to this body?" She said, "Girls trip." At the end of chapter six I told you Jane visited a psychic. This demon disclosed when, where and how which was later confirmed by Jane. As this demon rolled her hips and waved her hands in the air, she seemed to be gaining strength or energy. In her menacing old lady tone what came out of her mouth next rattled me. She said, "Demons are all in the house. Demons in four corners of every room." She then started speaking to other demons asking some, where were they going, telling others to come here. I could not see the demons but Ivy and I could definitely feel the presence of the demons. The room temperature was getting colder and the atmosphere was filled with intimidation and fear. I knew we could not allow fear to paralyze us so we both started speaking in tongues, praying in the Holy Ghost! If we did not change the atmosphere, we would have been overwhelmed by darkness and hell. Our home had become like a demonic amusement park. I said to the spirit, "Where are the demons and who are they?" She responded by saying, "I know not what, who do you think I am, I know not work for you!" I commanded this demon to leave the room. She responded saying, "I not go no where!" Under the anointing and power of Christ, I grabbed Jane's wrists. The spirit then buckled in pain as though fire was shooting throughout its body. The demon then said, "Okay I go, I go." When the demon stood up it slumped down, with Jane's mid-section pushed forward, her shoulders and chest slumped back with her arms dangling by her side, it then turned Jane's feet parallel. As she walked, her toes were pointed out meaning her feet were sideways, almost turned completely backwards. She was literally walking with the inside of her heels dragging each foot forward.

Our house is ranch style so everything is on the same floor. When we left the bedroom and stood in the hallway connecting all the other rooms, this demon called Sorcerer stood still and laughed saying, "They are running, they run, they know you coming, they scared, you come they go." I begin to anoint each room and pray. When I got to my son's room the demon stated, "They hiding in a corner and on ceiling." I realized that what my son saw was real! When I went in my daughter's room the demon said, "They under bed hiding."

Because what we were seeing and hearing was so unbelievable Ivy decided to get her phone to secretly video what was happening. She would purposefully lag behind, walking intentionally behind the demon. She knew that often times in doing deliverance I recorded audio and video as proof but I only sought to do it under the direction of the Holy Ghost. As she started to record, after about 15 seconds the demon turned around and snatched the phone out of her hand saying, "You record me, you recording me! No recording me, I tell Jane she no trust you!" She held the phone in the air squeezing it with both of her hands. She then slammed it on the counter and said, "Footage gone!" When Ivy looked at her phone the footage was erased. When we got back to the room I proceeded with deliverance commanding Sorcerer to leave Jane's body and the atmosphere, commanding angels to drag the demon to hell! The spirit immediately left but I knew there was a greater problem. I had demons in my house.

The next 48 hours would prove to be super intense. That morning as usual we were up at 6:30AM taking the kids to school as if nothing had happened that night. We had gotten only a few hours of sleep. Our life was not normal. We were literally living between two different worlds. As a pastor and first Lady people still came to us with issues and problems in need of direction and prayer. But no one had a clue about what we were dealing with and going through.

The next day was quiet. We were all tired and Jane never got out of bed. Usually after deliverance her body needed time to recover. She would sleep and rest upwards of 10 to 15 hours straight. That night everyone needed to go to bed early. About 8PM I proceeded to put the kids to bed. Again, my 2 1/2 year old daughter was extremely restless and I was painfully tired unable to decipher if she was being stubborn or being irritated by demonic spirits. Ivy could not deal with her so I had to remain in her room for over an hour while she cried and refused to go to sleep. At around 10PM, I got frustrated and demanded that she go to sleep. I laid her in her bed and left the room exhausted. She continued to cry for about 15 minutes then she got quiet. I got in the bed but before I dozed off completely I decided to go check on her one more time (With my eyes swelling with tears

I continue to tell this story). I quietly walked down the hall not wanting to wake her up. When I got to her door I heard her saying over and over, "Get away from me, get away from me, leave me alone!" Instead of barging in I decided to peek in the room. My baby was on her knees, at the end of her bed, with her fist balled up, punching at the air saying, "Get away from me, leave me alone!"

This is my innocent baby! Oh God, my baby! My baby! My little girl! (Please forgive me as I write through my emotions.) I went in the room grabbed her and hugged her saying, "I am here, Daddy and Jesus will protect you." (God, help me get through this chapter). As I prayed, she fell into a deep sleep. I laid her down, shut her door and declared, "You will not have this room or this house. I started anointing the walls and everything in the room praying in the Holy Ghost. I went back to the bedroom with all types of emotions running through me. I was initially upset that God was allowing my child to go through this but before I even got to the room to tell my wife what was going on God spoke to my spirit and said, "Your daughter will be a warrior. Your son will be successful as well but your daughter will carry your mantle. Hallelujah! Hallelujah! God told me, "Son you feel demons and you feel my presence but your girl, going on 3 years old can see demons and see my presence! She is not afraid to fight!"

When I got back to the bedroom I woke Ivy up and told her about what I saw and that our little girl would be alright. Over the next weeks, I put them to bed with worship music and scriptures playing all night long and throughout the day. I determined, decreed and declared any demon living in this house would have to get saved!

Let's pray: God I thank you that you never leave our side and that even in the darkest situations you are a very present help. It was David that said in Psalm 139:

"O lord, thou hast searched me, and known me. ² Thou knowest my downsitting and mine uprising, thou understandest my thought afar off. ³ Thou compassest my path and my lying down, and art acquainted with all my ways. ⁴ For there is not a word in my tongue, but, lo, O Lord, thou knowest it altogether. ⁵ Thou hast beset me behind and before, and laid thine hand upon me. ⁶ Such knowledge is too wonderful for me; it is high, I cannot attain unto it. ⁷ Whither shall I go from thy spirit? or whither shall I flee from thy presence? ⁸ If I ascend up into heaven, thou art there: if I make my bed in hell, behold, thou art there. ⁹ If I take the wings of the morning, and dwell in the uttermost parts of the sea; ¹⁰ Even there shall thy hand lead me, and thy right hand shall hold me. ¹¹ If I say, Surely the darkness shall cover me; even the night shall be light about me. ¹² Yea, the darkness hideth not from thee; but the night shineth as the day: the darkness and the light are both alike to thee. ¹³ For thou hast possessed my reins: thou hast covered me in my mother's womb. ¹⁴ I will praise thee; for I am fearfully and wonderfully made: marvellous are thy works; and that my soul knoweth right well. ¹⁵ My substance was not hid from thee, when I was made in secret, and curiously wrought in the lowest parts of the earth. ¹⁶ Thine eyes did see my substance, yet being unperfect; and in thy book all my members were written, which in continuance were fashioned, when as yet there was none of them."

Notes

Chapter XII

Queen of Hell

Considering all we experienced over the past week, we decided to sit Jane down in hopes of getting more specifics about her trip and visitation with a psychic. She discussed how the psychic spent longer with her than any of her girlfriends, almost two hours. She could not remember everything that took place. She did remember this older woman was clinging to her and hugging her in and unusual manner, saying how special she was. (To take over the life of a devout Christian would be a great prize in Satan's system). Jane said the woman drew something on her back but she wasn't quite sure what was going on. After speaking with her, I was reminded of my first encounter with the woman I spoke of in Chapter 7. This woman also visited a psychic. It's amazing how God will take you right back to the test you failed and give you the opportunity to pass. Having a better understanding of Jane's situation I knew exactly what I was dealing with and what needed to take place in order for Jane to be completely delivered.

If you can recall, the deliverance with Ivy began when she disclosed information she had covered and kept secret most of her life. Speaking her truth, she literally uncovered and exposed the demons that were hiding in the darkness. In like manner, as Jane began to speak her truth disclosing her faults, mistakes, purpose for going to the psychic and what happened while she was there. She was exposing the very demon, the witch that was seeking to hide behind the many strongholds she invited into Jane's life. After the conversation Jane started to unravel. Instead of going to her room, she went and laid across our bed, it was about 11PM. The next two days would be the most difficult of my life.

We followed Jane into the room, she started crying saying "I'm so tired, I'm so tired, and I don't want to do this anymore!" I started praying a normal prayer of comfort simply asking God to keep her, encourage her and bless her. As I continued to pray she became increasingly intolerant of prayer. After about 20 minutes she started moaning and scratching her body. She went to the opposite side of the bed and faced opposite me. I walked across the room to the other side of the bed to face her. She crawled across the bed to the opposite side. I said loudly, "Speak your name demon, I command you to look at me and speak your name! She refused to face me. I then decided to get on the king sized bed. The spirit fully manifested and started cussing me out. By this time I had been cussed out so many times the words meant nothing. The demon finally turned around and looked me dead in my eyes sitting in the middle of the bed. I started praying in the spirit knowing that this would start to irritate the demon. As I prayed, this demon started speaking in Latin! Fluent clear Latin! The louder I prayed the louder it prayed seeking to drown me out. This went on for about 15 to 20 minutes. I then started quoting scriptures. Every scripture I started to quote this demon would finish the scripture before I did!

As the demon kneeled close to the end of the bed I went to place my hand on Jane's head and the demon knocked my hand away. Ivy got down on her knees in the corner of the room and started to pray. The demon started mocking saying. "You don't know what you're doing." The demon started praying louder attempting to discourage her. Then on all fours this spirit launched itself off the bed directly where Ivy was positioned and said, "You scared b****! Ivy then raised her voice loudly saying. "I rebuke you in the name of Jesus!" The demon started laughing and repeating her saying in a squeaky voice, "I rebuke you in the name of Jesus, I rebuke you in the name of Jesus, I rebuke you in the name of Jesus." At this point I was starting to get visibly upset and went and got an anointed bottle of water. The demon looked at me and said, "You getting upset Marky, you getting mad Marky, what are you going to do, you going to sprinkle some water over me?" That's exactly what I started doing thrusting water into her face. I would say, "Fire in the name of Jesus!" "Fire in the name of Jesus." Initially, it seemed as though it had no effect on this demon but after about 10 minutes you could see that this spirit was feeling the burn. As I thrust the water the demon started trying to avoid the water shifting positions and putting its hands up to guard itself. I said, "Speak your name now! In the name of Jesus, the son of the living God who gives us authority to cast out demons, I command you to speak your name!"

By this time two hours had gone by and I had gone through a whole 16 ounce bottle of anointed water. The demon refused to give a name. I asked Ivy to get another bottle of water. The Spirit of God told me to put water on my hand and place my hand on Jane's back. As soon as the water and my hand touched her back the demon begin to scream in agony! With my hand on her back controlling the actions of the demon I said again, "What is your name?" The demon spoke a name that I cannot remember. I do recall it was the name of the witch that gave power to the psychic that Jane visited while out of town. After naming itself the witch manifested. She got on her knees in the middle of the bed, stretched both hands to the air, lifted her head up and started saying, "Come, come, come, come, come, come, watch the show, you sit here, you sit here, you sit here, you sit here and you sit here." For 5 to 10 minutes she literally gave demons direction positioning them around the room. I immediately felt the Spirit of God come over me. As this witch summoned demons, I started to summoning angels. I started giving God praise saying. "I bless you! I praise you God! I magnify your Holy name. You are worthy to be praised from the rising of the sun to the going down the same! You are Holy! You are righteous. The king of kings and the Lord of lords! When praises go up blessings come down!

You said, the angels of the Lord encamp round and about them that fear him! Send angels now to fill this room! Let your glory fill this room! Let your anointing fill this room! Let your power fill this room! Let Heaven fill this place!"

Child of God, you could feel the presence and power of God taking over the atmosphere. I knew without doubt angels were in the room fighting, slaying demons, chaining demons, sending them back to hell. The atmosphere changed and the demons that were summoned and positioned all around the room were no longer there. This witch was slowly losing her power. I then said, 'In the name of Jesus, I command you to leave this body." Screaming she said, "No!" I put water on her back and started rubbing my hand from the top of her shoulder to her lower back. The demon was hollering in agony. The Spirit of the Lord spoke to me saying her back is the portal through which demons had been entering. Immediately, everything made sense. The psychic drew a pentagon on Jane's back during her two hour visitation.

Pentagon: "A reversed pentagram, with two points projecting upwards, is a symbol of evil and attracts sinister forces because it overturns the proper order of things and demonstrates the triumph of matter over spirit. It is the goat of lust attacking the heavens with its horns, a sign execrated by initiates."[13] The flaming star, which when turned upside down, is the hierolgyphic [*sic*] sign of the goat of <u>Black Magic</u>, whose head may be drawn in the star, the two horns at the top, the ears to the right and left, the beard at the bottom. It is the sign of antagonism and fatality. It is the goat of lust attacking the heavens with its horns. In short, it is used by devil worshipers to summons demons and acknowledge the devil.

I continued laying hands on her back and head saying, "Angels drag this demon to the pit of Hell." This witch replied, "I am dying, I am dying, I am dying." In the spirit, I could see the psychic that got power from the witch was in physical pain. The witch that gave her power was dying; losing her grip on Jane's life. After a few more minutes of prayer, there was a loud scream and the witch was gone. Jane then started to speak as usual saying, "What's going on, what's going on, what's happening, why am I all wet?" Ivy immediately said "It's not her, it's not her." Jane said, "Yes it is, it's me, it's Jane. I was thinking what do you mean it's not her. Ivy looked at me and said again, "Its not her!" I started to pray in the spirit. I looked directly into the eyes of Jane and said, "In the name of Jesus speak your name!" All of a sudden, the demon started laughing mocking me saying, "You fool." I said again, "Speak your name!" Without any reservation this demon said, "I am the queen of hell." I started to pray in the spirit and after about ten minutes she just laid down. Jane's body could not take anymore. It was like this demon just disappeared allowing Jane to return to normal. Over five hours had passed. We were all tired and literally fell asleep in the room together.

As discussed previously, in Satan's kingdom there is hierarchy, a chain of command. Even though no demon wants to leave its home, the job of the little demons is to protect the strongman, the head of the family. The job of the strongman or stronghold is to protect the dominant power whether that be a witch, sorcerer, queen or the devil himself.

It's too much to explain every experience but I specifically remember one deliverance session when one spirit that was cast out of the body was fussing at another spirit that was still in the body saying, "I thought you said we would be safe here. You are going back to hell with me. You are about to be put out too! You are in trouble! We will both smell the pissy black roses

95

of hell." Demons that do not perform well or carry out their duties are actually tortured in hell. The reason why demons fight to live in people, fight to remain in homes, and fight to keep their territory on earth is simply because they don't want to be in hell themselves. And if demons don't want to be in hell, I sure as hell, don't want to be in hell!

The next morning we all woke up late, including the kids. It was Saturday. Thank God! I asked Jane how she felt. She said, "I'm doing okay, just tired." When one has been completely set free from demonic forces they are not devoid of energy. When you have been set free completely, you are re-energized, reinvigorated, enthusiastic and ready to take on life. Demons suppress and drain, making their victims sluggish and unenthusiastic. I am telling you the demonic weight must be lifted in order to be free. I could tell Jane was still heavy and needed deliverance; however, Ivy and I had to spend the day with the children. Jane did function that day. She worked on projects and cleaned up. Even though she was not feeling well, she decided to press her way through the discomfort. That night I knew I could not do any deliverance. I was mentally drained still needing to prepare for Sunday. The next morning we all got up, had breakfast and went to church. Throughout the service I would look at Jane. I could see she was out of it, just going through the motions, not engaged in the service at all. The power of God was present in the service and was irritating, stirring up that demon still in her. When the service ended, we headed back to the house trying to just be normal. Jane knew her body was still under attack. She was literally zombie like, unable to function. We all agreed that once the kids were sleep, we would continue with deliverance. I was tense and anxious throughout the rest of the day. Like a boxer one hour before the big fight I had nervous anticipation. When it's all said and done I may be anointed by

God to do this work but I'm still just an anointed human being. It is important for pastors to know we are not invincible. Even Jesus got overwhelmed in the Garden of Gethsemane anticipating the cross.

(John 26:39) "And he went a little farther, and fell on his face, and prayed, saying, O my Father, if it be possible, let this cup pass from me: nevertheless not as I will, but as thou wilt."

In no way am I comparing myself or my situation to that of Christ. But I do want you to understand, just as Christ had to depend on God in the most difficult season of his life, we too must depend on God and His Word in our weak moments, knowing and believing that his strength is made perfect in our weakness. Our faith is not proven when everything is going wonderful, when all the bills are paid, when the relationship is on cloud nine, when the children are on track, or when our enemies are at peace with us. Rather our faith is proven when we have the ability to praise God in spite of our affliction knowing what the enemy means for evil, God will turn it around. In essence, whatever doesn't kill you is only there to make you stronger. Your strength is in your ability to humble yourself and depend on the Lord.

(Corinthians 12:7-10) "And lest I should be exalted above measure by the abundance of the revelations, a thorn in the flesh was given to me, a messenger of Satan to buffet me, lest I be exalted above measure. [8] Concerning this thing I pleaded with the Lord three times that it might depart from me. [9] And He said to me, "My grace is sufficient for you, for My strength is made perfect in weakness." Therefore most gladly I will rather boast in my infirmities, that the power of Christ may rest upon me. [10] Therefore I take pleasure in infirmities, in reproaches, in needs, in persecutions, in distresses, for Christ's sake. For when I am

weak, then I am strong."

In this passage, Paul learns to praise God in his weakness knowing that it affords God the opportunity to show up and be his strength making a way out of no way. Again, as I anticipated deliverance to take place that night. My flesh was weak but my spirit through Christ was ready for war!

At 8 PM, we put the kids to bed. Jane became more and more irritable by the moment. Remember, demons are not stupid. They are very alert, some clairvoyant and calculated. Jane started to say all the things we heard before such as, this is stupid, I'm fine, this isn't working, I don't care anymore, etc. It was not her. Demons know when there is a threat of eviction and they will do all they can to avoid the process. Before Jesus cast legion out of the man that lived in the tomb, there was a storm on the sea. When Jesus got off the boat he delivered this man and left.

(Matthew 4:35-39) "On the same day, when evening had come, He said to them, "Let us cross over to the other side." ³⁶ Now when they had left the multitude, they took Him along in the boat as He was. And other little boats were also with Him. ³⁷ And a great windstorm arose, and the waves beat into the boat, so that it was already filling. ³⁸ But He was in the stern, asleep on a pillow. And they awoke Him and said to Him, "Teacher, do You not care that we are perishing? ³⁹ Then He arose and rebuked the wind, and said to the sea, "Peace, be still!" And the wind ceased and there was a great calm."

(Matthew 5:1-5) "Then they came to the other side of the sea, to the country of the Gadarenes.[a] ² And when He had come out of the boat, immediately there met Him out of the tombs a man with an unclean spirit, ³ who had his dwelling among the tombs; and no one could bind him,[b] not even with chains, ⁴ because he

had often been bound with shackles and chains. And the chains had been pulled apart by him, and the shackles broken in pieces; neither could anyone tame him. ⁵ And always, night and day, he was in the mountains and in the tombs, crying out and cutting himself with stones."

After the calm, the boat arrived and Jesus was met by the man with Legion. Jesus was intentional about getting there to deliver this man and the enemy was intentional in causing a storm to prevent his arrival. The devil does not want God's people to be free. Freedom is knowing that you do not have to live bound. "Whom the Son has set free is free indeed!" The enemy comes to steal, kill and destroy but Jesus said I have come that you might have life. That word (life) in John 10:10 comes from the Greek word "Zoay" which means life to the fullest.

I refused to give up on this young beautiful girl until she was completely free, ready to walk into her destiny and live life to the fullest. At around 10 PM, we were finally gathered in the room and ready to go. After about 15 minutes of praying in the spirit, the queen of hell emerged. I went through the same process. I asked, "How did you gain access to this body?" She responded by saying, "The devil gave me access you fool! Do you know who I am? I am the queen of hell. I will never leave her. She has too much power she knows too much!"

I told Ivy to grab some anointed water. My plan was to use the same method torturing the demon into submission. I started to thrust the water into her face with my fingertips saying, "Fire in the name of Jesus!" After about 10 minutes she said, "You stupid f***, this feels good, give me more." Even though it did not seem to phase this demon I continued sprinkling and praying in the spirit knowing that demons like to bluff and can fake pain. When I got to the second bottle of water, the demon started to attack me and Ivy personally. This demon called out all of our faults, failures and weaknesses. Matter of fact, during this time we were having some financial struggles. The demon literally tried to cut a deal with me. In a savvy like street tone the demon said, " What do you need Mark? You need some money? How much do you need $1,000, 10,000? I can get you whatever you need." She then targeted Ivy jumping to the end of the bed saying, "Boo!" Ivy was a bit startled and the demon started laughing saying, "You're scared, Oh, you are scared. I can see it in your eyes, you're scared." At that moment I started mocking this demon laughing saying, "No you are scared. Demon you're getting ready to lose your home. In the name of Jesus you are coming out tonight!" I asked Ivy to grab more water. As Ivy started to walk away, the demon decided to take things to another level. The demon said, "How are the babies? Oh! They look so cute while they sleep." This was initially upsetting because we knew spirits were trying to irritate our children and had been for weeks. Instead of getting the water Ivy detoured to go check on the children. Without even being able to see Ivy, the demon said, "Awww, she's going to check on the babies. Look at her. Ain't she supposed to be getting water pastor?"

At this point I was starting to lose my cool. With the water I had left, I grabbed Jane by the arm and placed my other hand on her back saying, "Fire in the name of Jesus!" The spirit growled in pain. I knew I was headed in the right direction. Ivy came in and handed me the water bottle. As I was getting ready to pour water into my hand to put on Jane's back, the demon grabbed the water bottle and crumbled it with one hand. Ivy then got another bottle. This time we began praying in the spirit, quoting scripture, asking God to send Angels! The situation was so bad.

100

Even though it was close to 2AM, I was ready to call a pastor I knew over to help out. The spirit wouldn't let me. For some reason this experience was for us only. I continued to apply water where the pentagon was drawn on her back. In agony, the spirit continued growling and pushing me away. This back and forth tussling went on for over an hour. Eventually after more praying in the spirit and giving commands in the name of Jesus, there was a loud scream and Jane fell and laid still on the bed. Jane said, "What's going on, what's happening, I feel better. Pastor Mark thank you so much! We all hugged each other in disbelief.

After the hug, Jane sat down on the bed. When she sat down I noticed a belly button ring. It looked like a silver claw. The spirit of the Lord told me, "Tell her to take it out." I said. "Jane, sweetie, I need you to take the belly button ring out." I turned to Ivy and said, "Please help her get the belly button ring off." Jane stood up in defiance and with her normal voice said, "I don't want to take it off. There is nothing wrong with me having a belly button ring. I have stopped drinking, smoking and everything else. I'm not taking it out." As she proceeded to walk out of the room I stood in front of her and said, "Jane, you must take it out. God is telling me it is an access point for the devil." She said, "Please stop, I am fine! I am not the devil! This is me. I just want to go to my room. Please get out of the way!" I said, "Jane, it's not that you can't have a belly button ring, you can get another one." "It cost too much," she said. "Whatever it cost we will get you another one. Let's just please take that one out." Not having any other sensible recourse, she sat down and said, "Okay, but I'm getting another one." We said, "No problem at all."

When Ivy reached to help her get the ring out the queen of hell reemerged laughing and cussing. That's right! For ten minutes, she literally used Jane's vocal chords to sound just like her but it wasn't her! Even though several hours had passed I was reinvigorated thinking that once the ring was out this would end. I also knew this demon was tired; faking strength it did not have. She stood on the bed saying, "The devil is mad, the devil is mad now, the devil is coming, the devil is coming, he is mad!" I said, "In the matchless name of Jesus Christ! God has given his Son a name that is above every name, that at the name of Jesus every knee must bow, every tongue must confess, things in heaven on earth and under the earth! In the name of Jesus whose blood was shed on Calvary for the remission of our sins who rose on the third day with all power! And the same power that raised him up dwells on the inside of us and in that power I command you in the name of Christ, the Son of the living God! Come out! Your time is up, Come out!"

As she was standing, I put my hand on her stomach and on her back simultaneously pressing in hollering, "Come out! It was like the demon was getting hit with a sledgehammer over and over. The queen of hell fell down to the bed. After hours of hearing prayers and scripture, she was weary, worn and exhausted. As she turned her head back and forth in agony, Ivy and I proceeded to take the ring out of Jane's belly. When we finally got the ring out there was a weak cry out. Jane looked like she was dying, but it was the demon dying. I said, "Angels drag this demon in chains to the pit of hell never to return to this body again! In Jesus Name!"

It was over! The real Jane started crying uncontrollably saying, "I was hoping you would not give up, I knew what was going on the whole time but I could not do anything. I was suppressed just hoping you would hang in there and you did. Thank you, thank God! Thank you Jesus! Praise the Lord!

Let's Pray. God save me and fill me with your Holy Spirit! I believe in Jesus, His life, death, and resurrection. I thank you that today is the beginning of a new season. A season of power, victory and breakthrough! Be glorified in my life and let your perfect will be done. In Jesus name! Amen

Notes

Chapter XIII

Take Authority!

Let's re-establish some facts to make sure we are on the same page and in position for deliverance and power! First, you must know without a doubt that Satan has a kingdom and he is the prince, president, dictator and ruler of his kingdom. Just as it is with the military and government, Satan's kingdom is orderly, sophisticated, strategic, and operational. For example, the U.S. military consist of the Army, Marines, Navy, Coast Guard, and Air force. In like manner Satan has demonic forces that are specifically assigned to the air, airwaves, oceans, seas, continents, nations, countries, states, cities, counties, neighborhoods and streets that make up the world in which we live. His mission and plan is found in I Peter 5:8, "Be sober, be vigilant; because your adversary, the devil, as a roaring lion, walketh about, seeking whom he may devour."

Remember, his operation is covert, he doesn't want you to believe that he is real. Satan would prefer that you believe he is some fictitious character that walks around in a red jump suit carrying a pitch fork. The truth is, his kingdom is very much alive and active in our everyday lives. His spirit is in the TV shows, movies, videos, music, books, games, toys, drinks and drugs. I have delivered people that had demons enter them through music from artist who have given their soul to the devil. I could name three artist that have won just about every music award possible but get their power, influence, fame and swag directly from hell. The enemy uses their influence to create perversion, sexual immorality and addictions amongst their fans. Their victims end up trying or doing exactly what they hear and see from the celebrity. In many cases of deliverance I commanded demons to tell me how they entered. As a result, I was given the artist name. In some cases, the club, concert, or the place where they were listening to the music and the specific song they enter through! This is not to say that every secular artist belongs to the devil or every time you watch a movie or listen to a song you are in danger of being possessed. It is dependent on your covering and level of anointing in your life.

I have also delivered children as young as five years old. I won't say that they were possessed but they were under constant attack. These kids were constantly having nightmares, experiencing random pain and dealing with extreme behavioral issues. The attacks started after watching animated movies thought to be innocent by the parents, or by constantly playing diabolical video games infiltrated with blood, creatures and violence. So now that we understand in part, Satan's operation and purpose let's move on to our power and authority.

(Matthew 11:12) "And from the days of John the Baptist until now the kingdom of heaven suffereth violence, and the violent take it by force)

(Matthew 16:18) "And I say also unto thee, that thou art Peter, and upon this rock I will build my church, and the gates of hell shall not prevail against it."

(Luke 10:19) "Behold, I give unto you power to tread on serpents and scorpions, and over all the power of the enemy; and nothing shall by any means hurt you."

Collectively these scriptures tell us God has given us power and expects us to use that power to push back the gates of hell, take back what the enemy has stolen and take authority over our lives. Your question may be how exactly do I do that? It starts with accepting Christ into your heart and believing in his life, death and resurrection.

(Roman's 10:8-10) " But what does it say? "The word is near you, in your mouth and in your heart; that is, the word of faith which we preach. 9 that if you confess with your mouth the Lord Jesus and believe in your heart that God has raised Him from the dead, you will be saved. 10 For with the heart one believes unto righteousness, and with the mouth confession is made unto salvation."

Once you are saved you must then activate your power. Remember, (Ephesians 3:20) "Now to Him who is able to do exceedingly abundantly above all that we ask or think, according to the power that works in us,) Through prayer you must seek God with your whole heart and soul earnestly asking him to fill you with the Holy Ghost. When God was calling me into ministry, He allowed everything around me to fail pushing me into his will. I decided to read the Bible for 30 days committing to walk in obedience doing everything the word instructed. I started in the New Testaments with the book of Matthew reading a Bible I could understand. During this time I developed a hunger and thirst for God that could not be quenched. Every day from 4 to 6 hours a day, I was locking myself in my room. I would get down on my knees and pray asking God to fill me with his spirit. After the third week of praying and seeking God as the song says, "Something, something happened and now I know he touched me and made me whole." After about 15 minutes into prayer He filled me with the Holy Ghost! I am constantly asking God to refill me again and again so that I maintain the power to deliver others as well as myself.

Beloved you have a treasure in an earthen vessel! Greater is he who is in you! You can do all things through Christ who strengthens you! Life and death is in the power of your tongue! God has giving you dominion and authority over this world and Satan's kingdom! Take authority over your life! Take authority over your home! Take authority over your children! Take authority now! If you keep on doing what you have always done you will keep on getting what you have always gotten! This is your season to breakout, breakthrough and become all that God has called you to be!

Let's pray. "It is no secret what God can do what He's done for others He can do for you." God, I thank you for the person who has read this book. I pray that they have been enlightened, encouraged and energized knowing that there is power in the name of Jesus. The weapons of our warfare are not carnal but mighty in God for the pulling down of strongholds. The battle is not yours it belongs to the Lord! In the name of Jesus, you have the victory!

Notes

Conclusion

While writing this book, I experienced spiritual warfare but it was expected. I knew the enemy would do anything possible to prevent the writing of this book. However, God's Will has prevailed!

My children, even though they had traumatic experiences, for several months, were oblivious to what happened over the course of nearly three years. Today, my son is 5 ½, my daughter is 3 1/2 and they are doing very well. My daughter, Zion likes to get up and pray with us all every morning, and demands to say the grace first at every meal.

Ivy is preparing to enter into a season of ministry where she completely avails herself to God ministering her story to women across the world letting them know you do not have to live in secret, in bondage or in pain disclosing that the same God who set her free wants to set all free who believe and have faith.

Last, but not least, Jane. After the last deliverance Jane experienced many rough days and attacks. Even though she was freed from hundreds of demons and the queen of hell, she realized she needed to be filled with the Holy Ghost and had to read the Word daily.

She is now working again and in a great relationship with a God-fearing man that supported her through our struggles. While doing deliverance, we learned through the power of the Holy Spirit that Jane was to write her own book and that her story would minister to the masses! My prayer is that she finds the strength, confidence and fortitude to finish the book she has started writing, walking in the power and anointing the devil himself sought to ruin and kill.

As for myself, I look forward to sharing my gifts and my

story with all who will receive. Through the power of Christ, my job is to equip saints, expose the darkness and push back the gates of hell!

Prayerfully, one day I will get to meet you the reader.

References:

"Pigs in the Parlor," The Practical Guide to Deliverance (Paperback), by Frank Hammond, Ida Mae Hammond

"Prayers That Rout Demons," by John Eckhardt

"A Divine Revelation of Hell," Paperback –September 1, 1997 by Mary Baxter

"Understanding the Purpose And Power Of Prayer, by Dr. Myles Monroe, May 1, 2002 Whitaker House.

George Barna reports.

The Christian post

NKJV Bible

Wikipedia, the free encyclopedia.

About The Author

Pastor Mark A. Couch was born in Philadelphia, PA in 1974, and raised in Atlanta, GA. He has a heart for people; known for making others feel welcomed and unjudged. Pastor Couch has the unique ability to inspire, encourage and motivate those who have given up on life, church and God.

Pastor Couch received his Bachelor of Arts degree in Biblical Studies from Carver Bible College, a Masters of Christian Education from Luther Rice University, and completed graduate studies in Israel. He is currently a full-time pastor and founder of Life line church in Fairburn Georgia, Chaplain for the Fulton County Sheriff's Department and CEO of "S.H.I.F.T Teen Movement," a faith based non-profit organization that partners with the Georgia Fulton County School system to train and transform troubled youth.

Notes

CPSIA information can be obtained
at www.ICGtesting.com
Printed in the USA
FFOW03n1738190817
38919FF

9 781936 937967